SUNDAY

SUNDAY

A Minister's Story

John C. Harper

Little, Brown and Company — Boston – Toronto

FIRST EDITION

T 08/74

Library of Congress Cataloging in Publication Data

Harper, John C
    Sunday: a minister's story.

    Autobiographical.
    1. Harper, John C. I. Title.
BX5995.H33A35   289'.092'4 [B]   74-4401
ISBN 0-316-34709-4
                        HARPER

Published simultaneously in Canada
by Little, Brown & Company (Canada) Limited

PRINTED IN THE UNITED STATES OF AMERICA

Some said, John, print it; others said, Not so:
Some said, It might do good; others said, No.

— The Author's Apology for His Book
(Introduction to *Pilgrim's Progress*
by John Bunyan)

To the four
who live with me all day on Sunday:
Debby, Jeff, Betsy,
and especially
Barbie

Preface

WHEN MY FRIENDS heard that I was writing this book, some of them were brave enough to ask me why. I think there are two answers. At least these are the answers that I give myself. There may be others, but I don't know them just now.

First, I've long wanted to write about the ministry as I personally have lived it. Mine has, I realize, been a limited experience. I have no illusion that it is novel or unique. But life during the last twenty years — and even before that, when I was growing up in my father's rectory in Massachusetts — has been for me a fulfilling one, which I would like to share with others.

My second reason for writing *Sunday* is harder to

put into precise words. It has more to do with people's feelings in general, less with the ministry — much less my ministry — in particular. For I've wanted to write about Everyman (to use the fashion of medieval morality plays) — about what happens to all men and women as we grow and wonder, as we face the joys and sadnesses, the victories and defeats that make up our quite ordinary lives.

Granted, I have written about these feelings from my vantage as an Episcopal minister. That is the only vantage I have. But I am talking in *Sunday* as much about people who are lawyers or housewives, insurance brokers or stenographers, as about the profession I myself happen to represent. If you see yourself, your family, your friends in *Sunday*, then the book will have been worthwhile.

Obviously a lot of people have had a hand in preparing *Sunday*. Some, like my wife Barbie, my former secretary Rosemary Hutchins, and John Turnbull, a colleague at St. John's Church, have read drafts of the book and have given valuable help in preparing the manuscript. Even my three children have gotten into the act, mostly to complain that there's not more in the book about them. (I take that back. They really have given me useful suggestions.) My editor, Llewellyn Howland III, has, among other things, given moral support, encouraging me to say what I mean and to try to say it simply.

But of course there are literally hundreds of people who've had a role in making *Sunday*: friends and parishioners from the early days of my ministry; the members of St. John's Church at Lafayette Square in Washington, who've put up with me for ten years and who've given me much more support than ever I deserved; more particularly the Vestry of St. John's, fourteen men and women who allowed me to go on sabbatical when this book was being written (and to travel to such diverse places as Bermuda, the Holy Land, Italy, and Cape Cod.) No minister is more blessed with a parish and lay leaders than I am at St. John's.

These people I thank, as I thank all whose lives I've touched and who have touched and so wonderfully enhanced my own.

SUNDAY

Chapter 1

SUNDAY MORNING, seven o'clock, is the strangest hour of the week. For most Americans it doesn't exist at all; it's the middle of Saturday night or the end of it or the time you get up to go the bathroom before going back to sleep. But for a clergyman seven o'clock Sunday morning is the beginning of his hardest working day. You know the old saying about how the minister is incomprehensible on Sunday and invisible the rest of the week? Well I'm sometimes both incomprehensible *and* invisible. I've been a minister for twenty years and I can never get used to waking up on Sunday and, when my head clears, wondering what it's all about.

Sometimes I think I'm invisible as well. Invisible

to my wife on the other side of our king-size bed. Invisible to some of those people who during the next five hours at church will get me confused with God. There are times when I'm even invisible to myself. For like my wife and my parishioners, I often wonder who I am and whether I, John Harper, may really be God after all.

Sunday morning at seven is a lousy time to think about these things. Who really cares what I feel about myself when I get up at seven o'clock for the early service at church? I do. That's who. Part of me — the part that's married to Barbie — wants to go back to bed, to sleep, or to make love. This is the elemental, simplified man who got married twenty years ago and has helped to raise three children and likes what my mother used to call the creature comforts. The other me is paid to get up and go to St. John's this morning at eight o'clock, engage in a liturgy which strangely draws me into its comforting arms, and meet people as pastor and sometimes as friend. This me is an Episcopal priest, now rector of a prestigious parish in Washington, D.C. The man and the priest are often at lonely war with one another, and at no time more than this Sunday morning, when the lighted dial on the alarm confirms the truth of the bell's insistent ring. It's time for the bodily man to get up and for the priestly man to go to work.

Only the bodily man doesn't want to get up. He never does; he's afraid. And that's partly what this book is about: the fear of being human and what happens to that anxiety when it finds itself wrapped up in a person who happens to be a minister — or to use the technical word in my Church, a priest. But it's mainly about the man who, as I said, is married to Barbara, wakes up on a dreary Sunday morning in a king-size bed, and wonders who he really is. All this may be, and I hope is, about a minister too, but it begins with someone who's in his late forties, who has gotten gray on top and perhaps somewhere inside as well, and who asks a lot of questions about himself in order to find just a few of the answers. The priest sometimes helps with the answers, but only when the man inside me asks them first. Maybe you know what I mean.

I read an article somewhere about the difference between the characters of the Japanese and American people which seems to me to be relevant at this point, at least so far as my own life is concerned. According to the article, the Japanese think of themselves primarily in their social roles, as husband, son, employer, worker. The American sees himself as a personality first who just happens to have one of these roles from time to time or for a limited purpose. He is first of all a man and secondarily a personality who functions, often uneasily, in some relationship or in some job.

I'm more an American than I know. Certainly the character of the Japanese as it was described to me isn't my role model. The more I think of myself and what I do, the more I realize how important my "core personality" is. It's that which says to me at seven o'clock Sunday morning: Harper, old friend, watch out. They'll try to clobber you at church today, on the street this morning, maybe here first at breakfast. Better be sure of yourself and know who you are. Then that me which struggles with my weight and a slight headache this morning, and with some misgivings about my self-honesty replies: O.K.; you're right, but maybe I'll learn something today I don't know about myself — and about the priest as well.

For some reason I woke up this morning remembering an anonymous letter I received on Friday. I dislike anonymous letters, and yet in spite of myself I always read them and worry about them afterward. If you want to hurt someone send him an unsigned hate letter, implying that everyone feels the way you do. That'll get to the gut every time. Friday's letter wasn't as bad as some. Ministers seem to be fair game for people who want to vent their anger and frustrations, and a minister, of course, because he's a man of God, is never supposed to fight back. Especially if he doesn't know who's sore at him.

Friday's correspondent described herself as "a lady who longs to return to St. John's." She began by saying she has no idea what my plans for the parish's future are but that she hopes I'll pay more attention to Christ and less to social issues, the "world outside" she called it. What does she think I've been talking about these last ten years if it's not God, or Christ or Jesus or whatever name you want to give to Divinity?

Just because every sermon isn't filled with a lot of pious (to her? to me?) words or phrases, doesn't mean it's not deeply or at least partially Christian, as much Christian as a human mind can make it. Where is her Christ if not in the city of Washington, in the eyes of people like her and me, in all the fuzzy relationships we engage in? Christ: she missed him because she doesn't want to meet him, and as I put on my clerical collar, look at my clerical self in the mirror, I take some comfort in the fact that I'm right and she is wrong. Only she doesn't think she is wrong, and if I have to admit it, I'm not so sure I'm all that right.

That's why her letter gets to me, hurts in the way she knew it would. The letter shouldn't be as much on my mind this morning as it is. The woman won't be in church today anyhow, if she's still longing, as she says, to "return to St. John's Church." She's probably making some other rector's life miserable or else she's at home feeling sorry for herself for losing Jesus.

Besides I've got other things on my mind today. The weekly sermon which I wrote two days before I received her letter and which has enough flattering references to Jesus Christ to satisfy a Southern Baptist. A conference with a young couple who want to get married. A cocktail party with a lot of older people who probably won't have been in church and who, while not missing Jesus Christ in a sermon, are nevertheless suspicious of me and of whatever liberal tendencies I may show. And some hospital calling,

7

which I try to do Sunday afternoon, because when I'm tired I'm most apt to be quiet and listen to people who want to talk.

Oh yes. I forgot, too, that I'm going to stand before five hundred people, spill some of myself to them in a sermon about uneasy relationships, let them take a good look at a proud, sensitive, ambitious, anxious minister who sometimes drinks double martinis, who doesn't always say his prayers, and who's often terribly alone. Some of these people I'll greet at the door of the church after the service, wearing what my younger daughter Betsy calls my minister's smile. Some I'll be glad to see, because they bolster not just my ego ("What a lovely sermon; I cried and cried") but support my need for friendship. Others I'll wish would drop dead then and there — right in front of me on the church steps. I'll smile at them too even though I won't mean it, and they'll smile too — I hope — and whatever Church means to us both will be all mixed up with our feelings about each other, about what we are, about what we'd really like most to be.

I live a mile and a half from St. John's, which is across from the White House on Lafayette Square, and I like to walk to work, especially on Sunday. It gives me a chance to come to life, to get my body and mind in working order. It also gives me the opportunity to sort out some of the feelings that wake up with me. Today is one of those gray, in-between days in the city. The sun is supposed to come out later

8

this morning, the radio says, but so far the best thing about the day is that it's cold, raw, and damp, and that's not much to start off with. Connecticut Avenue is empty except for a police car (which passes without any obvious interest in me) and two brotherly old drunks heading for the cheap all-night diner for the fifteen-cent coffee served in Styrofoam cups. An elderly Irish maid who works in one of the houses near ours also meets me, but we avert eyes as we have for almost ten years now. She, I suspect, is on her way home from Mass at the nearby Catholic church, and either thinks I'm a Catholic priest whom she mustn't speak to or else she knows damn well who I am and doesn't think it worthwhile acknowledging the minister's smile I used to give her when we first met.

The police car, the drunks, and the maid represent some of the people I know best. That's oversimplifying it, of course, but it's one of the things I think about as I walk to church this morning, an idea that comes into my mind and which keeps me going for the half hour it takes to reach St. John's. The policeman reminds me of all the people who pass by and don't really give a damn, even though they're mostly good people, going about their work or whatever it is they're doing. It's just that they're involved in their own lives and I in mine, and unless some kind of crisis occurs we won't ever really meet. I like police-men in the way I like most of the people I meet in the course of the week who have no interest in the church. There's something about them which I envy. They get along perfectly well without those reli-

9

gious props I find so necessary. They seem so secure in what they're doing, so sure of themselves as they ride past me. It's as though they are insulated from the pressures which are a part of my life on foot on the street this morning. The policeman in the cruiser is part of a world which has no need for the Church, for religion as I know it anyway, or for me.

I don't like the two drunks, the unshaven derelicts who live together in some room off Connecticut Avenue and are either just getting up or just about to go to bed. I've seen these two off and on for the past couple of years. I don't like their life touching mine. In a way, I suppose, their very frailty reminds me of my own, their shabby life a reminder of what I might become. They stand, or fall, outside the society of which I'm a part, broken people who enter the diner to get coffee and a morning fried-egg sandwich to keep them going. Like the policeman they don't care about me, don't notice me any more than the Irish maid on her way home from Mass does. But I am terribly aware of them. How can I avoid this, when they tell me of my own humanity, my own failures and need? How can I ignore those who intrude into an otherwise peaceful Sunday walk and whose irregular lives are set against my own?

They are found in all churches and synagogues. They are respectable, outwardly well behaved, but shallow in their religious commitment. They don't want to be disturbed by me — and I may not want to disturb them. But I know that this is only a half-truth, for the most conservative people in my congregation, the most seemingly indifferent people I meet on the street, have a great longing for someone to love them. They don't want to be disturbed, and yet they do; they don't want to be noticed, and yet how terribly much they want someone to care about them, to notice them when they're in church, to miss them when they're not, to speak to them on the street. And, brother, I know just how they feel.

I think about the policeman, the drunk, and the maid this dreary Sunday morning on my way to church. I remember that all of them, or rather people like them, will touch my life today. The indifferent ones will meet me as I, indifferent so often, will meet them, and we will pass by and pretend not to care. But it will matter very much to each of us that someone cares. The hurting people will come by, too, and they will bother me because I don't know how to relieve their hurt and because I too sometimes hurt inside and am in need of the same medicine they ask for, for which none of us has a name. The proud will come into my life, defenders of the status quo who are upset by all the changes of contemporary life, and I will find in their intransigence some of my own unbending, self-centered ways.

They will be there in church today. They will come, like me, for a variety of complicated reasons, and they will find there people like myself, composites of the indifferent, the anxious, and the apparently secure.

What have I got to say to them this morning that

will matter? What word for them? For me? If it's any good, it will have to be honest and it will have to begin with some understanding of the policeman who passes by in his cruiser with just a glance in my direction, with some compassion for my fellow derelicts, and with some willing confrontation with those who return from church, steadied by their exposure to what is holy and yet who have been unwilling to hear, much less to live, what they have been told is true.

Chapter 2

WHAT DOES A MINISTER do on Sunday? I eat a big breakfast, have a sandwich at suppertime, watch the "F.B.I." and maybe a late movie, and then go to bed. In between I spend about five hours in church. I may have several drinks in the evening and maybe one at lunch, although as I get older — and I hope wiser — I may cut out the booze altogether and try to deal with my anxieties in some other way. Because Sunday is a day of anxieties, very complex ones in fact, and I need all the help I can get to deal with them.

Like prayer. That, I suppose, should be the number one item on my list of emotional first-aid equipment, and in a way it is. Only prayer takes many different forms, all the way from getting down on my knees, and when I pull myself up again thanking God I can still get upright, to conducting public worship and wondering what time the Redskins' kickoff is this afternoon and whether I'll be through church in time for the game.

As I say, prayer runs all the way from the solitary to the social; it may be very formal and precise: "Dear God, please keep Mrs. Arlatt off my back this morning; don't let me forget to thank Cookie for arranging the flowers; and, please, let the choir sing better than they did last Sunday." Or it may be the same thoughts couched in less traditional forms, like wondering if there's any help for the precocious third grade kids who signed a petition not to have any more Sunday School.

Prayers like those, formal and informal, occupy much of any clergyman's morning, and by the time evening comes spirituality will take a slightly different form, either thanksgiving for the good things that have happened ("Thank you, God, for letting me hold my tongue when Hortense Tooley took me to task for forgetting to call on her aunt") or prayers of confession and contrition ("I'm sorry, God, that I blew up at Hortense Tooley but she's bugged me long enough; she expected me to know her aunt was sick when no one ever told me; and I'd just finished dealing with Mabel Richardson, who expects me to heal her broken little finger.")

Amen. Amen.

That's the way I spend my Sunday: eating, drinking, and making merry with my friends and with

God. For Sunday is a very merry time indeed. Fun for all hands — for those who are out to get the minister or one another, for those who want to get in a word with God, for those who've come to see what the rest of the parish is up to. It's merry too because Sunday is supposed to be a feast day, a festival. And so people come in their best clothes, and several hundred of them, or maybe a good deal fewer in some places, band together to sing "Praise God from whom all blessings flow." It's fun time for all, except that not everyone looks as though he's having fun. You'd think a rousing hymn which thanked God for blessings — and anyone in church should be able to make up some kind of list for himself — would be sung by people with happy faces. Not so. Many of them don't sing at all, and some of the rest who do sing that familiar Doxology do so as though both the tune and the words were thoroughly distasteful to them. Perhaps they are, and perhaps the minister needs to take this into consideration when he plans his Sunday and contemplates what he's going to say to his fellow worshippers.

Because that's just what they are on Sunday, the minister and the people in the pews— fellow worshippers. For five hours on Sunday I meet a variety of people — "all creatures great and small," as the Sunday School hymn would have it — and when I forget, as I sometimes do, that we are in this together, I'm lost. Then the Redskins or anticipation of the "F.B.I." take over and the church service becomes what it's always in danger of being, a performance by an actor who may be second- or first-rate depending on how well he's learned his lines.

That kind of church service is a farce, and no one knows this better than the minister as he stuffs himself at breakfast on his wife's scrambled eggs and bacon in order to get enough physical strength to provide the emotional strength to get through the rest of the day. Because working in a church demands gifts not even St. Paul knew about and certainly ones he lacked. It requires patience and yet openness to change, a genuine love for people and yet some understanding of what makes them tick so perversely, a desire to serve the Lord and yet a recognition that service is probably done in small ways rather than through the grandstand play.

One trouble is that churches actually have grandstands, and the preacher is right up there, in spite of knowing better, from the very start of the morning. He mounts the pulpit, and the only way he can be stopped during the next five hours is for his good sense to assert itself and tell him to come off it. Some would say this differently and say it is the Holy Spirit who thus speaks; they would also remind the parson that it is not just his word but God's that gets spread around in the church. Good sense. Holy Spirit. Call it what you will. It is nevertheless God who comes up beside that man in the pulpit and in one way or another (and those ways can seem underhanded sometimes) God takes the most insensitive of us and tells us where to go.

Sometimes, of course, God lets us get into trouble

on Sunday, maybe for years of Sundays, before He gives us the word. You can be a minister and not know anything about God at all, and it's very humiliating to wake up after you've been leading public worship for a number of years and discover you've been doing it all wrong.

Well, better late than never. The Bible is more concerned over one sinner who repents than over four hundred and ninety-nine Episcopalians whose incomparable liturgy has already saved them. And so the minister no less than his most profligate parishioner needs to be saved, and while Sunday morning is often inconvenient for him, what with conducting church services, relating to Hortense Tooley, and hushing a noisy acolyte in the chancel behind him, it is as good an opportunity as he'll have to be saved from sin.

Sunday is the time for conversion, too, in spite of many distractions. Self-examination takes place for the parish priest even when he's eating that big breakfast, even as he walks to church, even when he relaxes with his family, even when he goes to sleep. Yes, and even when he's in church, trying to sort out in his mind the difference between the human and the divine and to decide which legitimately should claim his attention at any given moment of the day.

When I was a little boy, in age as well as in mentality, I loved to walk with my father on summer Sunday mornings, while he prepared his sermon. I think he must have done some preparation the night before, but he was a last-minute kind of person and enjoyed saying what the Spirit prompted him to say. Unfortunately, he didn't say it awfully well. Public speaking wasn't his long suit. My father often prepared those sermons while walking in the local dump, a journey I especially enjoyed since, in case others haven't known it, dumps are the most exciting places of discovery for young boys and for homiletical preparation for middle-aged clergymen. My father's rule was that during the time we were within the confines of the dump I was to remain silent, or at least not bother him. Was he praying for divine aid for his forthcoming sermon? Was he trying to remember the three parts of the sermon which in his study on Saturday night had seemed unusually effective and sure winners for Sunday morning? Was he thinking, by way of relaxing his mind, of the hobbies which would later occupy his time?

I don't know. Maybe it was a combination of all three, because his sermons were a mixture of holiness that lay beyond anyone's experience, a few challenging ideas that had earlier occurred to him, and a good many references to his outside interests— such as making wooden animals out of birch logs for the children of the parish.

My father's sermons had a little bit for everyone: holiness, ideas, and Ralph Harper. Those dump sermons were a kind of summary of what Sunday was to my father. They weren't all worship or all thoughts about religion or all fun and games; they were a combination of the three. That, I suspect, is what Sunday is intended to be for the clergyman, if only he will believe it and if only his congregation will let him make it so.

Do the parishioners expect an unusual degree of holiness from their captive holy man on Sunday? Then let them see him when he carouses with his family, when he kicks the family dog, when he can't sleep on Sunday night for being so keyed up. Do they expect him to go full tilt on church business all day? Then let them see him when he relaxes for a while after church and then when later he makes the rounds of the hospitals and visits people who aren't interested in his morning's sermon but in getting well. Do the minister's friends see primarily a human individual before them on Sunday, someone they've spent Saturday night with or someone they know has feet of clay and sometimes a head and heart made out of the same material? Then let them see him before he goes into church, before he enters the pulpit, when he stands at the door of the church after the service to greet the flock, and they will see another man who for a little while at least has been humbled by the immensity of the opportunity and by the continued failures to measure up to what for him would be his best.

People in church see all these things in their minister, and they are, I think, just as confused about him as he is about himself. They know about the breakfast and the supper and the late-night movie, because they know he must be human in spite of occasional evidence to the contrary; they know he prays out loud and talks to them about God, because when they come to church on Sunday morning they hear his strong voice. They know he runs an institution, because they see proof of it around them when they enter the church door and are given a Sunday bulletin. They hear the organ, and they look at the physical evidences of divinity before them.

But in understanding these things they may not fully know the man who is a part of them. He's had a hard time getting out of bed this morning and he will have a restless night again tonight, and in between he will try to be himself, for their sake and for his own. When he's not on camera and no one else is listening, he will add "for Christ's sake" too, without being at all irreverent.

He begins his day thinking about the things he has to do and he goes to bed on Sunday night remembering the things he's left undone, and unless he's one of those relaxed characters who can turn everything over to the Lord for ultimate approval he feels a nagging guilt at his omissions and his obvious failures. He remembers the people who were in church that morning, and in his mind's eye as he tries to go to sleep he sees some of them, expectant or dead to the world and to God, eager for some new truth to break in upon them or else uncaring and indifferent. The minister's Sunday night is a welter of emotions.

Not all of them are negative ones by any means. I've had some success. With old Mrs. MacKenzie, for instance, who loves me for whatever I do and who once confidently told me, "Every sermon you preach gets better than the next." Mrs. MacKenzie and her middle-aged bachelor son are my fans and I secretly look for them in the congregation on Sunday morning. "We're all in our places with bright smiling faces." So are Prill and Len Dodson. A year ago when it appeared that their six-month-old baby was dying in Children's Hospital I spent hours with them in the baby's room. One Sunday I was there a good part of the day, leaving only to return to St. John's to conduct the eleven o'clock service. They hear what I'm trying to say when I talk on Sunday about how God is found in relationships with each other; sitting in the balcony of the church they look down at the chancel and know what it means to have a minister stand by them when they need him the most. Sunday service is for them the culmination of a lot of what else Christianity is about, and if I have a hard time getting to sleep on Sunday night I can remember Mrs. MacKenzie's frothy enthusiasm for me as a man and the Dodsons' gratitude for me as their priest.

Mrs. MacKenzie and Prill and Len Dodson are in every parish, and so are the other people who are committed to the Church. There is nothing unique about St. John's nor about my ministry. I've seen myself in scores of other clergymen as they conduct services on Sunday morning, and when I've sat as a visitor in the congregation of other parishes I've seen the ghosts of all the people I know by actual name within my own church.

Last year on a vacation in Bermuda I went to one

of the Church of England parishes on Sunday, and came away realizing that in many ways I'd seen the worst and the best of institutional religion. Here was a replica of an English country Gothic church plunk in the middle of Bermuda, as out of place on that lovely island as the Church of England service, which was deadly and dull by anyone's standards. The words were read uncomprehendingly by the high voice of the English parson, the language itself that of another time and place, the music unbelievably inappropriate. The sermon was mercifully brief, almost as if the minister assumed that no one was listening to what he said. Indeed, he appeared as bored in delivering it as some of us in the pews were in hearing it.

But was that all? I don't really think so, nor do I think the small congregation, mostly of older people pretty well divided between black and white, was uniform in their boredom or their lack of interest. The vicar was a man before he was a priest that morning, and whatever faults he might have in his professional, priestly role, it was not for us to judge him as a human being. Like me, he is probably a mixture of things both good and bad, of failures and of hopes. I saw in him, as I listened and watched and tried to pray, the all-too-human figure who stands at the altar of St. John's and at other churches on Sunday morning and asks somehow to be used by God.

Perhaps that Bermuda vicar would have been a stronger man if he had been in another profession. Possibly someone else could have reached more of the members of the congregation than he did. Maybe another would have given a more forceful exposition of the Gospel so that people's hearts would have been set on fire. I'll never know. I only know that this was the man who was there that morning. He was chosen to be the expositor of "Good News" for me and for the fifty other people who were in the same church with him. We had no other choice at that moment than to accept him for what he was.

This is the way the ministry always comes out. People are asked to take the man for who he is and allow him to do his best. It may never be sufficient for some of us and indeed he may never reach many people, only Mrs. MacKenzie maybe and occasionally a Prill and Leonard Dodson and their baby. But that is enough. He is not God; he can only do what he can, and if he looks beaten down and is often ineffective, it may be comforting to him to know that other clergymen have failed too, that those who worship with him on Sunday morning have in their time and in their own way known the bitter taste of defeat. The occasional mountaintops are of course what make it all worthwhile.

One Sunday night in my first parish I received a call from the police that there had been a drowning at a nearby lake and would I come because the wife of the man who drowned asked for a minister. Of course I'd come. I got dressed and drove several miles to the small lake, which was edged by cabins belonging to people who lived in Boston and who went out there on weekends, mostly to fish. I'd not been to the lake before and consequently had trouble finding the exact road which led into it. Eventually I found what I was looking for and got out of my car and edged my way through a small crowd of people, mostly black, who were standing around the body of the man which had been dragged from the lake. The chief of police stood beside the man's distraught wife, and as I came up beside them in the glare of the headlights from several cars which ringed the scene, I felt every eye upon me. The woman sobbed as she mutely pointed to her dead husband who for some reason hadn't been covered but instead was lying there, eyes open and staring at us as though those car headlights were as intrusive to him as they were to me.

The woman and I knelt down and I put my arm around her. There wasn't much else I could do. I had no idea what to say. She and her husband had been visiting relatives who owned one of the fishing camps, I was told, and had gone out in a canoe at sunset, and when the canoe suddenly capsized the man, who was a nonswimmer, drowned while his wife managed to hold onto the boat until help came. Now their life together was suddenly, cruelly ended; she was a widow without warning, alone there with the body of the man she had loved for what I gathered had been a long time.

Strangely enough, I had never been faced with a sudden death before. I didn't know exactly what was expected of me. The curious around us waited for me to say something. After all, Reverend, that's your job, they seemed to be saying; that's why we sent for you.

"Depart out of this world, O Christian soul," I began, remembering vaguely words from the Prayer Book, "in the name of God who created thee, in the name of Jesus who redeemed thee, in the name of the Holy Spirit who sanctifieth thee." And then for good measure I added "and may thy rest be in Paradise this night." I wasn't sure then, and I still don't know, where Paradise is, but I hope it is some place other than that muddy bank with a grieving woman who had just lost her husband and for all I knew her worldly security as well. I hoped and literally prayed that God would somehow do for two people, a man and wife, better things than I could know or pray for then. It all seemed so useless with those silent people standing around me, as I knelt beside the black woman and as Benny Cartwell, the police chief, cleared his throat as if to say, "OK, let's get on with it. Move the body."

The wife and I weren't ready for that or for any ending to her grief. We somehow were there together, two people who had never met before and who would probably never see one another again. But the death of her husband brought us close and her grief became mine just as I hoped that my prayer might reach her.

Rest in Paradise? Certainly there was no visible paradise there that night; only the summer's dark and some car lights to relieve it, and the silence of con-

25

fused and curious onlookers who only heard a woman's cry and a minister's prayer and who must have known that both were very much the same, that cry and that prayer.

Years later I was at Walter Reed Hospital when a ninety-six year old woman, who had long been a member of St. John's, died. During lengthy illnesses the doctors had kept her alive until there was really not much body left. She had literally withered away. When I went to see her in the intensive care unit, as I had each day of the previous week, it was obvious that the end was very near. She was barely conscious, enough though to recognize me and to take my hand. Together we prayed, only it was she who whispered the prayer as she had so often to me before, this old lady whose faith was so much stronger and more noble than my own and who on various occasions had shown me the meaning of a religion which not only had guts but which was graced with mercy and forgiveness as well.

For five years she had given me her friendship, and when she knew that she would not recover from this final illness she began to talk about the joy which she'd known in this life and the joy she looked for in the next. Lying there in her bed at Walter Reed, holding my hand with a grip of expectancy and hope, she began quoting those familiar words; "May I depart, O Lord, out of this world. . . . May my rest this day be in Paradise." And she closed her eyes, and as I watched and silently said the words of Committal, that Christian woman died.

But the black woman beside the lake: what did I give her in that moment when I tried to pray? The ugliness of death was present in her tears and in my own. I hope that after all these years that sorrowing wife knows something of the faith which most of the time passes my understanding and yet which must also be mine in words and sometimes in actions to give to others.

Chapter 3

WHAT MAKES A MAN a minister, or what happens when he stops being just a man and becomes a man who is a priest? A couple of years ago before a wedding I was to perform at St. John's I talked with the bridegroom in the vestibule while we were waiting for the bride to arrive. He was going to enter medical school and I asked him why he had decided to be a doctor. His reply startled me. "I don't really care about medicine as such," he answered. "I've decided I want to work with people. So I'm going into psychiatry. It seems to me the best way to help people. But I guess I have to admit that it's going to be a pretty hard grind in medical school, not having any interest in medicine."

I've wondered since about that bridegroom. The ministry never occurred to him as a possible profession. Here was a bright, intelligent young man who, in order to achieve perhaps the same end as a lot of people who enter the ordained ministry, was going to spend four, six years in a discipline that held no attraction for him. Why not seminary instead?

Some people would say that in order to go into the ministry you have to have a specific religious call. Maybe for some, but not for everyone. The Church is a much larger community than people sometimes think, and there is room in it for a variety of workers. I have to admit here my own prejudice, which might exclude the young bridegroom. The would-be minister has to have some curiosity about religion. I'm not sure he has initially to be curious about the institutions of religion, even though I'm sympathetic with one rector's surprise when a mother told him that her son was considering the ministry but he didn't like to go to church. Maybe that's all right, though, for the initial interest on the part of a young man or young woman may be only a vague surmise (a "clue," my father called it when I told him of my interest in going to seminary) that this profession is where he belongs.

I'm suspicious of anyone, ordained or otherwise, who has too many answers to intractable human questions or who articulates too readily why God is calling him to serve on a full-time basis among his fellow men. I'd rather see someone stumble around on the edge of things for a while, unsure of his calling and of himself, and gradually discover through a good deal of agony as well as ecstasy that the ministry is for him.

I went to seminary when I was in my late twenties with many misgivings, determined to try it for a year but maybe no longer. Field work during the summer and on weekends, the friendship of faculty and fellow students, and the gradual unfolding of the usefulness of the profession in a broken, disordered society all helped to convince me to come back for a second and then a third year, and then finally to apply for ordination. I couldn't answer very explicitly why I wanted to be a minister until I'd checked things out for myself and until I'd tested other possibilities.

Three years in the navy and four years of teaching in a boys' preparatory school in Connecticut helped to show me what I didn't want to do. I knew that I wanted to help people, and the other so-called service professions such as teaching or medicine didn't appeal. To put it in a slightly different way, I decided somewhere along the line that human lives have another side to them than the merely physical or the mainly intellectual. This dimension I began to call God. There is more to existence, I concluded, than "making" a one-dimensional living. All the struggling I and my friends were doing to keep our heads above water needed to be placed alongside that which does not vary with human success or failure.

I know this was a simple way of looking at God's

Grace; it was certainly a long way from a strictly Christian interpretation of human existence. But it was where I began, and from where I had to grow. I think I did grow, which is what the seminary experience at its best seeks to help a person do, and through the years there as well as within the ministry I have come to see that for me this constant search for truth is what religion is about. It is, you might say, the place where our pilgrimage meets that of Another who is searching for us. That juncture is filled both with great joy and great pain. It is never an experience, at least as I've known it, that is simple or easy, but rather one in which much is demanded of the searcher, and where his faults as well as his successes are mirrored against that other Searcher. But it is the best place I know to be in this life. I have welcomed being there to help others understand the dimensions of the human and divine encounters we daily make.

Here I am almost a quarter century later on a gray Sunday morning about to enter the glass front door of St. John's Church on Lafayette Square in Washington where I am the Rector. I, the ex-schoolmaster who was bored with "boiley boys" and wanted to work with different kinds of people, who went to seminary because I surmised there was something more to living than a comfortable existence within ivied walls, who got converted along the way, and who is responsible today for the religious insight of five hundred people who'll be in church — and another five hundred who won't. If I can reach some of those people then I'll be doing well for the Lord.

It's a tough business to be in. So many people expect God to stand up there in front of them, and while a few know without doubt that I'm not God (which is something I know too with increasing conviction), there are plenty more who'll make a serious mistake in identity and neither God nor I will have the heart to set them straight.

God has *His* reasons. *Mine* are that in spite of all the protests to the contrary, I often like the confusion in persons. There's something about playing God's part — the judgment, authority, power, that sort of thing — which is endlessly appealing to me. But God has other things to do too, like forgiving people and showing mercy and not letting His enemies get Him down. I don't do so well when I try to take on those attributes of divinity. Yet when I get dressed in my finest ecclesiastical garb and walk at the end of the choir procession, singing "Holy, Holy, Holy" (Who, me?), I really do enjoy what I'm doing, at the time anyway.

As I say, it's a good business, even though I've discovered it's really full-time, the pay's not all that great in spite of a ten percent discount on ferris wheels and at Brooks Brothers, and even though people make demands on you which never in a hundred years you can fulfill. Like the time pious, eager Rich Abbott asked at a Christian Education meeting what God's will for the Sunday School was, and I answered with assurance, until some more honest type broke up in laughter and told me to go to hell. I really thought for a second God and I were on the same wavelength and that I could speak authoritatively for Him.

Which is one thing the minister does try to do: speak authoritatively for God. It's risky, believe me. Three years in seminary teaches a man a good deal about the Bible, the history of religion, even theology, but that training — much of it really first class — doesn't give him enough insight into the workings of the Divine Mind. It may give him an inkling, through his study of history and other people's search for truth, of what the world of the spirit is all about, but he'd better beware of being too dogmatic at St. John's Church this morning or whenever he speaks in the name of organized religion.

People who write letters to the editors of religious journals tend to be very sure of themselves and of God. I envy them even if I can't speak so surely myself. A glance at the pamphlets in the tract rack in the vestibule of St. John's as I enter this morning tells me that most religious writers are divided into two groups: those who have the answers and those who are looking for them. We have both kinds of writers represented in our pamphlets at St. John's because in my own way I admire those people who can write firmly on, say, the Christian view of sex, without any of the ambiguities I feel in my own life, or about divorce or war when these are subjects I continue to change my thinking about and thus my public stand as well.

When I was first ordained I took a very rigid view about remarriage after divorce. I'd been recently married, and it was no wonder I didn't like to think seriously about what might happen if Barbie and I should separate. But as I've talked with couples over the years, counseled troubled marriages and been a part of separation and divorce between people who simply shouldn't stay together, I've changed my rigid position to a more flexible and I believe a more Christian one.

Once when I refused to consider presenting to the Bishop an application for remarriage, the would-be bridegroom stormed out of my office. "The hell with you," he shouted. "We'll find another minister. Every minister has his price." I suppose some do and will do literally anything for money, but I don't know many of them. The ones I do know are those, like myself, who've mellowed over the years, who've made compromises either because they've believed in them or because circumstances seem to warrant them and it's not been worth fighting every battle that comes along. But they've also tried to be men of integrity.

"Good morning, Dr. Harper," says the black Sexton, who's about to ring the bell for the eight o'clock service, which John Turnbull, one of my two assistants, is going to conduct. I like to sit in the back of the church for a while at these early Sunday services, count the house, see who's there, and ruminate about the rest of the morning. Arthur Butler has been Sexton at St. John's for a long time and he's seen ministers come and go. He knows how to keep us in line and he's not impressed by rank. Firmly polite, he appreciates what's fitting and what isn't. He's taught me things about weddings and funerals that only the wisdom of the years can give, in the way a fancy city undertaker once scorned my plan of riding in the hearse at a funeral by declaring, "That's country stuff. In this city the minister rides in a limousine!"

Well, as a matter of fact, I did just that at my first big funeral at St. John's when I was trying to establish myself as the new Rector who was knowledgeable in the ways of the world. I rode with several of the pallbearers in a large black Cadillac to Arlington Cemetery, and somehow in the city traffic between Lafayette Square and the Potomac River we got separated from the rest of the cortege. When we finally arrived at Arlington we could find neither the other cars nor, when we began to look for it, the grave. It was pouring rain and after driving aimlessly around the huge cemetery (I'd been lost in cemeteries before and should have known better), we found the gravesite only to hear the final words of the interment service, delivered by my predecessor at St. John's, who fortunately happened to be attending the service. It was humiliating, and as I walked up the slope to the grave, my shoes caked with wet, red Virginia mud, I wished I'd never heard of St.

35

John's or the ministry. It wasn't my fault; it was the chauffeur's; and after all, three pallbearers were late too. I could only mumble an apology to the widow, who I must say took it in her stride and has been a good and valued friend ever since. She perhaps would just as soon I had ridden in the hearse, but like me she was also probably intimidated by undertakers. They can be a formidable breed, and it's the courageous minister who crosses one of them.

Arthur Butler never has any trouble with undertakers or bridal consultants or even brides' mothers — or ministers. He just speaks softly, and if he doesn't actually carry a big stick, he holds the dignity of his Sexton's office over our heads, and we obey. When Arthur says good morning to me I know it's time to begin the working day and that he, on the stroke of eight, will begin it for me. It won't be Sunday until Arthur declares it so, and woe to the foolish minister who enters the sanctuary before that historic Paul Revere bell in the steeple of St. John's begins to ring.

It's comforting to know that Arthur's around. He gives stability to some things that the church is doing and he gives security to my life as I enter what's called the House of God and wonder if "He" will be there this morning. Arthur will be there, and that may be enough. My colleagues will be there too, but they're not God like Arthur is. They're like me, trying to discover the ways of speaking for God and they get as confused as I do. Only they have me over them and their personal God-search becomes sometimes incredibly confused.

It's a real problem for clergy to have two "bosses." I know, for I was once a curate. I was hired by a man who before I began work came through the receiving line at my wedding and asked if I couldn't start work two days from then instead of after the two weeks he and I had earlier agreed would be my honeymoon. Things went downhill from there. He departed on his summer vacation three days after I arrived, and the other curate and I spent the next two months rearranging the parish and the services to suit ourselves. This quite naturally displeased Dr. Moorman on his return from a peaceful summer in Vermont. His reaction displeased me, too. It somehow never got through my head that he was the boss and I was there, in chains it seemed to me at the time, to do his bidding. That year was often a nightmare, but I learned a lot, both from him and from the large city parish that Grace Church in Providence was.

It was my lot (among other duties) at Grace Church to conduct services in funeral parlors for the indigents who died in the city and who for some reason were buried by one of our clergy. I learned a great deal — which Arthur Butler years later has refined for me — about the funeral business from the sleazy funeral homes which overcharged poor people, including one funeral home that had hidden from view a lady harpist who wore the scantiest costume possible, to another which sold funeral clothes for the corpse that had no backs on the sequined dresses or the formal attire that Aunt Rose and Uncle Joe were garbed in.

I made seventy-five house calls one week just to prove to Dr. Moorman that I was working, and then Barbie and I slipped away to the shore for the next week while Dr. Moorman thought I was still hard at work, plodding along into homes where I probably wasn't wanted, burying Aunt Rose or Uncle Joe, and doing whatever unwanted chores the Rector had assigned his younger curate.

I hate to admit this, but I really did enjoy much of what I did in that first job in the ministry. But when a committee from a church in Foxboro, Massachusetts, came to see me I sensed happier if not greener fields ahead. I jumped at the chance to become Rector of St. Mark's Church, where I spent the next three and a half years and where our first two children, Debby and Jeff, were born. It was a love affair there between Rector and people, and we were sorry when the decision was made to exchange Foxboro, a homogeneous small town, for Bedford in Westchester County, New York, one of the most lush and comfortable communities I've ever known.

The two parishes provided good training for St. John's, which has a little of both Foxboro and Bedford in it. What it doesn't have in quite the same way is the intimacy of a community, where people know one another and where there is a common interest within the congregation. In Foxboro, and to some extent in the somewhat larger Bedford parish, I knew everyone in the town, most of the children by name, and a good many of the dogs and cats as well.

St. John's is different. This morning about one third of the people who come here to church won't be back again next Sunday. They're visitors from other parts of the country who've come to Washington and for reasons best left unsaid at this point have found their way to "The Church of the Presidents." Even among the rest of the congregation, the "paying customers," there is a wide variety. The city, no matter how hard I tried at first to reverse the fact, just doesn't lend itself to casual calling, and I spent the first years at St. John's trying to figure out how I could make this a family church and myself some kind of family minister.

In an ad in the local newspaper I'd once called the Foxboro parish "The Family Church," only to be taken to task by one of the spinsters in the congregation who wanted to know where that left her. St. John's has relatively few families and an inordinately high number of single people, but I still hope to make it a kind of community of people who come to know one another; I'm still looking for ways to make this come about.

Hope, you see, is the hallmark of the clergyman. If he didn't believe that something better than what he now knows is around the corner, he'd quit in discouragement. Whether it's more people in church, more committed Christians, more money in the parish till — whatever the need, he lives in hope that tomorrow the Church will come into its own and that it will be what he, for one, thinks a parish ought to be. Of course, like Charlie Brown when he misses kicking Lucy's football, he's bound to be disappointed. More money in the parish coffers for instance doesn't necessarily mean more loyal Christians. Each morning when he wakes up, the parson finds there are still fresh challenges and thus fresh hope.

Challenge and hope are the best words I can think of for St. John's as I come into church today. Even though I'm often discouraged by what I see and by what I try to do as the minister of this congregation, I'd never stay on here if I didn't believe that there were still people to be reached and that there were still some possibility of reaching them. In fact, as they say in church, the fields are ripe for harvesting — that is if the farmer's got anything to offer.

When I first went to St. John's a friend said to me: "John, you can preach heresy there, you can even be immoral if you want to, but for heaven's sake don't move the candles on the altar." He was partially wrong. You can't preach heresy and get away with it entirely. Nor is it possible to be immoral all the time. But he's right about the candles. Candles are what a lot of people care about, maybe sometimes even more than for theology or Christian ethics. I love to move candles, to make changes in the physical appearance of a church, and sometimes this has led to unhappiness, if not downright trouble. People care about what they can see and touch.

I remember in my first parish the altar rail, which I thought was hideous and wanted to do away with, only to discover that my good friend Ralph Lombardi had been confirmed at it and that for some reason it represented the place where he had met God. Result: no change in the altar rail. Or the time my minister father covered over an ugly stained glass window featuring an angel guarding two little children who were about to be eaten by a large snake. It turned out it was the favorite window of the Senior Warden, who said to my father that his whole religion was centered around that questionable representation of divine mercy. Result: the covering was removed, Mr. Everts's religion was restored, and my father said to himself, "What the hell, there will be time enough to make some changes." To prove it he stayed in that parish for forty years.

St. John's had what seemed to me a particularly unpleasant tile floor in the chancel before our architect, who was remodeling the chancel, covered the Turkish bath tile with a handsome red carpet. Result: my good friend Mrs. Simpson almost left the parish and for a year that was all she could talk about whenever we met. I don't say this was all she, or Mr. Everts before her, cared about. I do say that windows and carpets and changes in the arrangements of the candles mean a great deal to people, occasionally more than what the windows and the rest are supposed to symbolize.

St. John's is a hard church to make many physical changes in because it's a registered historic landmark and exterior changes in particular must be cleared with the government. St. Matthew's, Bedford, is also a historic church, in some ways lovelier than St. John's because of its setting on forty acres of handsomely landscaped land and because it has been less cluttered inside since it was built in the early nineteenth century. My immediate predecessor in Bedford (who was, like my father, rector for a long time) had had the courage and good taste to restore the church early in his rectorate. He had removed the ugly stained glass windows which the Victorian-minded members of the parish had so favored and installed clear glass which enabled the congregation to look outward onto God's handiwork while their bodies were inside listening to the preacher's. But Mr. Ketchum, alas, also liked a dark church, and so he installed permanent heavy blinds which darkened the interior and virtually shut out both the light and the sight of the attractive churchyard outside.

For reasons I've forgotten, I decided soon after going to St. Matthew's that the heavy blinds would have to go. I must have had some encouragement from the Vestry because I don't think I would have had the guts to go to the parish architect on my own and ask him to remove those blinds and to supply instead some graceful movable shutters that could be opened or closed at will.

I'll never forget my first Easter at St. Matthew's,

the first Sunday after the blinds had been removed, leaving the windows clear and open. Instead of the sun coming in to welcome that Easter Day, it was pouring rain outside as two hundred worshippers sang "Welcome, happy morning" and stared at the change that had occurred in the church since they'd last been there. It was light and airy, but it wasn't St. Matthew's as they knew it. I could imagine hostile glances throughout the service, and I couldn't keep my eyes off old Mrs. Merrill, one of the grandest grandes dames I've ever known, who sat possessively in the front pew, occasionally looking over at the opened windows and, so it seemed to me, scowling in disapproval at the callow new rector. I dreaded going to the door at the conclusion of the service. Moving the candles was nothing compared to changing the shutters.

Mrs. Merrill finally hove into view as the line of parishioners passed me, and I waited for the attack. "Young man," she said, "I've been a member of this church for a long time" — she didn't have to remind me of that fact: it was written all over her; it was *her* church, hers and God's — "and I want to thank you for taking those damn shutters off the windows. Now at last I can see what's going on in church, and besides I can do my knitting better during the sermon!"

Welcome, happy morning! Welcome, happy Mrs. Merrill! Welcome, movable shutters!

I didn't care if she did knit for her grandchildren and the prisoners of the local reformatory during

43

the sermon; in fact, I would have bought the wool myself if she'd asked me to. Someone liked what I'd done, and I'd gotten away with making a change. Mrs. Merrill didn't always agree with everything I did and she made it perfectly clear when she didn't. But when she was dying in a hospital some years later, she asked to see me and wondered whether instead of flowers at her funeral it would be all right if money was given to my discretionary fund. I knew then that I'd made it. She liked a young man who had the courage to move the candles and the shutters, especially when the shutters kept out the light which she needed for her knitting.

I doubt whether I would dare, even if I wanted to, take out the stained glass windows at St. John's as Mr. Ketchum did in Bedford. People like Miss Stancy are too attached to them. Miss Stancy told me once that a certain window was given in memory of her great-grandparents, who she added "were founders of St. John's, and I'm the sixth — (or is it the hundredth?) — generation to worship here." You can't fool around with founders' windows unless you're a bigger fool than I am. But I have to admit there are days when I'd like to try.

I did make a little chapel out of one of the transepts so that small services like weekday Communion Services can be held there. One old codger firmly refused to come to worship in the chapel, and another said to me when we held the eight o'clock service there on Sunday morning that it seemed to him that Sunday was no time to play around with second-best. Use the *big* altar, he told me, as though to indicate that only it could encompass the majesty of the Almighty and that my little side chapel would be an insult to the Sunday God.

The same old boy who refused to worship in the chapel at all withheld his hand when we tried to pass the Peace during a service. Ushers came down the aisle to take the hand of each person at the end of the pew, who in turn would take the hand of the person next to him. It's supposed to show our fellowship with each other, or at least that's what I told the congregation as I tried to get them to be more folksy. When the usher came to old Colonel Parsons and said to him, in proper liturgical style, "The Peace of the Lord be always with you," the unwilling and enraged Colonel snarled: "The hell it is," and kept his hand in his pocket. So much for passing the Peace.

Chapter 4

Wʜᴇɴ ʟɪɴᴅᴀ ᴀɴᴅ ᴍɪᴄʜᴀᴇʟ came into my office at ten o'clock on Sunday morning, I sensed that I'd seen them before. Only I hadn't. Linda's mother, a rich, attractive divorcée, whom I know as a casual Christmas-and-Easter member of St. John's, called me two weeks ago and said her daughter was engaged and could she be married at St. John's before Christmas. "It's such a dear little church," she cooingly said over the telephone, "and her grandparents as well as her father and I were married there. Even though Bill and I are divorced, I do love St. John's, especially for these family occasions. It's so divine." I let that last phrase pass; it was more accurate than Mrs. Bentley meant it to be.

Were Linda and her fiancé eager to continue this family tradition? I asked. The answer was predictable; yes, Linda did want a "church wedding" — of course she did, her mother said almost in disbelief — even though neither Linda nor Michael Laskey ever went to church. (And neither did her mother, I added to myself, as I told Mrs. Bentley that I would see the couple on Sunday morning after the nine o'clock service.) It's a hell of a time, I thought, to meet two people who want to be married in a pretty church just because it is expected of them, who will probably show up in blue jeans with no intention of staying for the eleven o'clock service, who will go through the motions with me for an hour and then depart, probably until the day before the wedding, when (if the wedding were going to be large enough, which no doubt this one would be, knowing Gwen Bentley), I'll meet them again. In the meantime, I'll forget their names, forget them, forget my own anger at them and at myself for letting the church be used merely to satisfy a mother's social ambitions for her daughter.

And Linda? Is this what she wants as she and Michael, a good-looking Yale graduate who has just finished Officers Training School at Quantico, come into my office? What if I told them, "To hell with all this nonsense. You don't care about a church wedding and neither do I, for you. Why don't you go out and get married at the District Court Building tomorrow morning, or better, I'll marry you right here, no religious words or anything, just pro-

47

nounce you man and wife." Isn't this what you want anyway, so you can legalize a relationship which (I suspect from some experience in these things) has already been well consummated?

Most of the weddings I've performed at St. John's in the ten years I've been here have been marriages of people like Linda and Michael, whom I've never seen before they arrive in my office. A city church is different from a suburban one where the minister knows the family, like a GP in medicine, and where he knows fairly well at least one member of the wedding party. I rarely know anyone. Not the bride. Not the groom, nor the ushers, nor bridesmaids. Often not the parents either. They come to a church like St. John's for a variety of reasons, some very complicated indeed, and some, like the ones I suspect have brought Linda and Michael here, not complicated at all. The church for many young people gives an echo of something in the distant past, their own as well as that of their parents, which is essentially good. Even though they may never darken the door of the church again, they can be mighty sentimental about a marriage service.

We've been experimenting with a new form of the marriage service; sometimes we even let the bride and groom write parts of the service themselves. But my own experience is that the further removed a couple is from traditional forms of religion in their daily life, the more conservative they tend to be when it comes to exchanging vows. They want the works: Lohengrin, white flowers, an aisle runner, Elizabethan words about the "mystical union betwixt Christ and his Church," and all the rest. Mothers aren't the only ones who like things the way things used to be. Brides, and grooms as well, go in for a lot that is traditional, just like the boys I used to teach in boarding school, who no matter how rebellious they might be when it came to serious theology always chose the most god-awful sentimental hymns to be sung in chapel.

I'd never seen Michael or Linda until they entered my office, but I'd seen others like them. I was prepared for an awkward encounter between two people who see the church as a nice pleasant setting for a nice pleasant wedding, who would be mildly miffed that I'd insisted on seeing them for a conference, who have their guard up for whatever personal questions I might ask them, and who are ready to tell me to jump in the lake if I — a minister, for heaven's sake — should ever take a strong stand about some of the things they want for their marriage. Like having Cousin Lucy sing a solo, or putting candles at the ends of the pews in a historic church across from the White House which might burn down at any moment and for which I'd be royally (that was a slip) blamed by all of Washington.

Isn't a minister supposed to be spineless, passive, and always agreeable? Isn't that the way he's pictured in the movies — a useless, but kindly, sort of ornamental person who for the most part speaks in Gothic letters and is presumed to have a Gothic mind?

When Pastor X steps out of bed,
He puts a neat disguise on;
That halo round his priestly head
Is really his horizon.

I've always been amused by these lines about the minister, although I'm afraid there's some truth in them for me as well as for others. A lot of people don't expect much more than limited horizons of the clergy; a lot of ecclesiastical and social history has seen to that. And to some extent that expectation has validity.

I could have told Michael that like him, I too had once been a young officer in the armed forces, that I had gone through many of the same intellectual and sensual experiences that he knows so well, that I too know what it meant once to go with my fiancée to see a minister about getting married merely because it was expected of us and not because I anticipated any significant help in my relationship to Barbara from an amiable man of the cloth.

I once had a young bridegroom in my office, in a similar interview. He had been up all night partying with his ushers, and for some reason for which I could now kick myself I waited to have an interview with the bride and groom until the day before the wedding. Mark was so hung over, and tired (and no doubt bored with me) that he closed his eyes, and before I knew it he was asleep in his chair.

My two Sunday morning visitors sat nervously on the sofa holding hands, as though to put up a united front against any intrusion I might suddenly make into their private life together. Why shouldn't they look at me with some suspicion? Their parents would have done a better job of talking to them about their future than I could. All I knew about them was that they came from middle-class proper-kind of families, that Michael (Linda's socially conscious mother told me this by way of a social recommendation) had gone to Yale and Columbia Law School, and was now a second lieutenant in the Marines, and that neither had any real connection with the Church or with St. John's. They were here because they were going to be married in a week (I had not been able to see them earlier because Michael had just graduated from Quantico and I didn't have the heart to make them wait until I, the great authority on marriage counseling, had seen them six times in deep sessions).

They wanted to get married, and I had had two weeks' notice from Mrs. Bentley, who didn't consider it necessary to tell me any earlier. If I didn't like them or they me, that was too bad. They'd now signed on. So had I. The best I had ahead of me now was to ask some questions (not really intimate ones, of course), decide what kind of people they really were underneath those nice middle-class good looks, and tell them what I think the Marriage Service is about.

Like telling them about how they really marry each other in the service, that I'm there to speak for their families and friends, and possibly for God. The congregation stands behind them, I say to them, literally and emotionally, and until he gives her away Linda's father stands between her and Michael. I tell them that when at the end I pronounce them man and wife I do so after reminding them of the things they have done in the service, of words and actions they have performed. They have ratified in the presence of a group of people their decision to be married.

We call that the betrothal and it comes at the beginning of the service, usually at the foot of the chancel steps when the minister asks whether they really do want to be married to the other. Then they make a sort of covenant between them, through the words of the marriage vow and by physically taking each other by the hand (the one sexual act we allow in church besides a kiss maybe at the end of the service), and they pledge themselves to each other for keeps.

I summarize all this at the end of the service, reciting merely what they have already said and done, and pronounce them husband and wife. Then, in my own right, I give the blessing, which I understand to be not that of the institution of the Church but of people, the ones who care about them and who stand as witness to the marriage or who, not present, nevertheless share their love with a man and woman. This blessing is really that of a whole lot of people, among whom I, in some ways, am the least important, since I may know them the least.

But I have been privileged to share in their most important moment — or at least so it always seems to me when I get to this point in the service — and I watch a bride and groom squeeze each other's hand, fondle the ring which has just been exchanged, giggle together over some secret joke, and maybe even shed a tear. I may not know them well, but in another sense I then know them very well, for I look into their faces at the end of the service, which no one else can do until they turn around and put on a public face for the benefit of their families, who broadly and approvingly smile as they come down the aisle.

I have seen something which is very private, which I often miss when the couple comes to my office ahead of time to talk about the wedding, when we sit and discuss what the whole thing means. I see earlier only an unwilling bridegroom and a sentimental bride who doesn't want any kind of contemporary liturgy or music that her mother and grandmother won't recognize as genuine wedding music. But later during the actual service I see the couple before me at the altar as a young man and young woman — sometimes old men and old women too having a try at it again — who may be saying to me that it could all be just a lot of words, who sometimes don't know why in the world they're in church, on their knees in a cutaway and a white dress, and yet who might also say — and I think very often too — that the words do reach. I hope Linda and Michael may be among these last; at least that's why I'm seeing them today.

I was prepared to be put off by Linda and Michael. After all, Gwen Bentley wasn't my most faithful parishioner and, besides, I hate to be used, whether as a minister or as a human being. But there was something very appealing about this couple as they sat in my office. I did most of the talking because I was conscious of the time. I really wasn't being fair to Linda and Michael but I had my own anxieties, such as worrying about the upcoming eleven o'clock service. Usually this hour before the main service is kept for the seminarians who work at St. John's, and I try to meet regularly with them at ten o'clock on Sunday morning, share my prejudices with them, and learn some new ones from them. I was aware that I'd had to cancel that regularly scheduled meeting with our three seminarians, one of whom is studying to be a Roman Catholic priest and who wants to learn how an Episcopal parish functions (he's learned a lot, and has given a lot to us, too), and I knew that the three of them were jealous of the time with me and jealous, in a way, of this couple who were usurping their hour.

Still, it was the only time I could see Linda and her fiancé. I had no other choice. Whatever pearls

I have must be given now, and anyway there were details about the wedding that needed to be dealt with. I had to lay down my ground rules about weddings at St. John's.

"Absolutely no pictures may be taken during the ceremony; this is a religious service, and it's disturbing to people. . . ."

"Flower girls and ring bearers give me a pain; they're unreliable and take attention away from the bride, but it's your wedding. . . ."

"Some music is simply inappropriate for the church; why don't you talk with our organist, Al Russell" (who, incidentally, will talk you out of your lousy taste), "and see if you can't come up with something a bit more appropriate; after all, the Wedding March in Lohengrin was written for a marriage that didn't turn out very well. . . ."

Etc. Etc. Etc.

I was running out of breath, and of ideas, and the clock which I can see from where I sit told me it was almost 10:45. Pausing, I noticed, and belatedly so, that neither Linda nor Michael was listening to me.

"Dr. Harper," Linda tentatively began, "there's something we need to talk to you about."

Oh God! She's pregnant and hasn't told me. They're being forced to get married here when they'd rather it was somewhere else. Gwen Bentley's gotten her big nose under the tent and is making them invite people they don't want. I've had enough weddings to think of things like that. Maybe Michael's been divorced. (The Episcopal Church until last year took a dim view of that to the point of making the poor couple go through the experience of applying to the Bishop for permission to be remarried and in the process digging up a lot of dirt from the past which often should just as well be left covered.) Is this what Linda was about to tell me?

"Excuse me, sir," Michael took over, "I think you should know that I'm Jewish."

Relieved, I quickly said, "That's all right; the canons of the Church require only that one person be baptized." As though that made everything all right for Michael and for everyone else who comes to the church for a wedding when perhaps they'd rather get married in a civil ceremony anyway. Was I trying to relieve Michael's conscience, or my own? Sunday morning was getting complicated, and I could hear the choir coming downstairs from the choir room to get ready for the processional into the church.

"I'm not a very good Jew," Michael went on, while Linda looked both defiantly proud of him and embarrassed at the same time. It was obvious that she adored him, but it was equally obvious that this was a problem that mattered to them both.

"I haven't been to synagogue for years, but my family and their friends are more active than I and, well, it would be embarrassing to have them at a service where Christ is mentioned so often, where everything ends with 'Father, Son, and Holy Ghost.' All the prayers seem to end with that phrase 'through Jesus Christ our Lord.' The service you've just described is very pretty, I have no objection to it really, and I know it's what Linda likes and what her family wants, but we've talked about this and, well, I'm uncomfortable with it. It's not the way I talk to Linda. I know I have no right to ask you to change anything for us, or for anyone for that matter. We'd like to get married in your church; it means something to Linda and it does to me too. But the Christian part of the ceremony bothers me, the words I mean."

Wow! Choir, here I come; wait for me; I'll catch up! Sing the first hymn through five times while I collect my wits and think of what to do!

Here's a fine young man who cares about his fiancée and for religion as he understands it, who's just thrown me a curve, and I don't know how to catch the ball. Why should I change everything I've just been saying to him about the meaning of this Christian marriage service simply because this boy with his Jewish background has to give in to his parents and their New York friends?

When you go to someone's house . . .

Why should he challenge me about what I believe about a marriage service, especially when I don't want to think about it now, or ever maybe, and when I can so easily throw the book at him and tell him this is the way it's going to be and if he doesn't like it tough beans.

After all, we do have standards, and I'm not going to be the pushover he thinks a minister will be.

But that's not right either. Michael didn't come on

that way. If anything he was embarrassingly polite, almost tentative in his request. Maybe I can get away with it and tell him gently that I have no choice but to use the Prayer Book Service as it is and that I hope he'll understand and hope that his parents will understand and hope that his Jewish friends will understand and hope that God will understand. Maybe I can kill him with kindness and he'll go along and not cause me any more worry.

"You see," Michael concluded, "I do believe in God and, like you say, about how He is present in our love for each other. I believe that Jesus was a good man, and all the rest about him. But I don't believe he was divine. I mean, I'm not a Christian. But I'd like to be married here if my religion can be respected for what it is and if I won't have to be hypocritical. . . ."

I've had all kinds of so-called Christian marriage services, from one in the Cathedral when the groom upchucked as he started through the door, to a ceremony in the garden of a fancy estate in the country where the cows, who ringed the lawn, had big bows tied to the bells hung round their necks. I've had marriages where the families weren't on speaking terms with each other, one where the bride actually backed out at the altar and fled home in tears, where a grandmother left the church in a rage because a black was in the wedding party. I've had lots of different kinds of weddings, even to several where the bride and groom have written prayers and one, even, when the bride's mother gave a prayer beforehand. Wedding services in the Episcopal Church needn't be so orthodox that nothing of the personality of the bride and groom comes through. I'm loath to flaunt my theological orthodoxy instead of looking for ways to reach out to others, to people like Michael who technically are not Christian.

Yet here I'd been going on about how the bride and groom really marry each other, that the wedding is theirs and not their mother's or their aunt's or the florists', and now I was caught in my own dishonesty when a sincere young man wondered whether every formula of the Christian faith has to be brought out in the brief service or whether his love for his bride couldn't be articulated in another way and still be said in an Episcopal Church. Can't there be words that do reach? Why not an Old Testament reading, or ending the prayers with the phrase "In God's name." Why all that business about the "spiritual union betwixt Christ and His Church"? If the service was edited would it be any less Christian, even though "God's name" might mean something different to Michael's family than it does to me?

Linda took Michael's hand again, and I was reminded of what other, far less mature couples, did at the conclusion of the service as they knelt before me. In these two people there was something sacramental, right there in my office. They were loving each other through some honest hard words and through the way they touched each other. If I said I couldn't alter anything, I guessed Michael would have agreed for Linda's sake. If I said I could make the changes he was asking for, I knew it would be all right with Linda. I didn't know what the Bishop or my colleagues would think of it. I had a fleeting, but strong impression of what many of the people in the congregation at the wedding would think, the traditional Episcopalians who might be shocked, some of whom would then whisper their racial prejudice to each other in the pews, "But you know, of course, that Michael's Jewish. Linda's such a lovely girl, but . . ." I could see it all in one of those flashes, but somehow I didn't care.

"Sure," I replied, "I think together we three can come up with a service" — I started to say "liturgy" but I didn't want to be churchy just then; I wanted to be a friend, to love them somehow — "which will say what you both want said. Not everyone will like it, neither your people, Michael, nor Linda's. But if it's what you want, that's OK, and I'm glad for your honesty."

And I'm glad that you, Michael, took me to task for all the claptrap I was giving you about marrying Linda, when all I wanted to do was to get my own way, to get this interview over with so I could go on with the morning service and my sermon, which all seemed at the time I planned them so much more important. I'm glad you made me think, for a couple of seconds anyway, what the Church is for — and what I'm for. Because you told me that the Church isn't an end in itself. You reminded me that I, the parish rector, am not an end in myself. We're in business to help people make some sense of their lives, and before we're through with this wedding I'm going to try to help you, Michael, and you, Linda, to make some sense of what this your marriage service is all about.

We're going to meet again, for it's time for me to put on the vestments of a priest in the Episcopal Church and try in the liturgy to be very orthodox. It's time to call it quits now, but we'll get together again this week and talk, not at each other but with each other, and maybe your marriage will get off to a better start because the Church and I care about you and not merely about our ecclesiastical niceties or our religious legalism. I've seen too many couples in this office who want to get it over with as easily as possible, and who'll never raise their doubts or ask questions.

I'm grateful for you, Michael, my friend, especially this Sunday morning.

Chapter 5

I HATED NOT TO MEET with Nick, Gerry, and Fred, our three seminarians. Sunday morning between ten and eleven is about the only time we have together, except in the actual church services. I like having contact with men training for the ministry. Over the last nine years I've had thirty-one seminarians working for me at various times and in various capacities. While they've been quite a crew, there's probably no more difficult breed of human being than someone studying for the ordained ministry. On the one hand, the reasons he's in seminary — to serve God and his fellow man — make him try very hard to do whatever his model of the clergyman suggests to him; on the other hand, the very intensity of the training puts him to the test and often brings out his worst as well as his best characteristics. I guess that's why so many seminarians today are wisely led into psychotherapy during their three years of training. It's a healthy thing that they are, both for themselves and for their future parishioners, although it's not always easy on the supervising rector, when the hostility and anxiety the psychiatrist's helping the seminarian deal with spill over onto others. On the whole, though, I respect enormously those seminarians and clergy who are trying to unravel the mysteries of the self so that they can be more effective counselors to others.

Thirty-one potential clergymen! It boggles my mind to remember some of them, those close to my own age who came from other professions to this peculiar form of graduate school long after their undergraduate years of academic training, and some directly from college, often with naïve expectations of the profession and of life.

Perhaps the hardest thing the men who've worked with me have had to learn is to make sense out of St. John's Parish. They see the Church in its most idealized and theoretical light, and they want to see a parish involving human lives on the most profound level. I, however, see these things happening in different ways, for most of our parishioners find their places somewhere along the edges and rarely in the center where the seminarian would like to put them.

One of the ablest men I helped train quit the program one day in disgust because he felt St. John's wasn't, as he said, "a Christian church." To him it was merely a collection of people who come here on Sunday morning, who don't know each other, and who aren't involved in anything more than, at best, weekly worship. He couldn't see the purpose of St. John's, and he wanted out. I tried to suggest to him that maybe there is more to people's involvement than he realizes and that it would be useful to him to analyze more carefully the rationale for a church such as St. John's. But he couldn't see it that way. He left, sadly, and for all I know is finding that St. John's-by-the-Gas-Station or wherever he's serving has some of the same faults that this St. John's has.

If nothing else, I hope that our men will become somewhat insulated by their experience here from a few of the disappointments that inevitably come along in the parish ministry when they're on their own. I hope they'll see all our faults, and be critical of them as only seminarians can be. But I hope they'll stick with the parish while they're in training in the belief that in the long run they may learn something here about the realities of parish life in the twentieth century and recognize the health that many parishes, including St. John's, possess. I don't want to dull their idealism, but yet I want that idealism to be tempered by real and not romantic expectations.

This is also true for assistant ministers, or curates, as they're often called. I've had seven full-time and a number of part-time assisting clergy, and they've been an unusually fine lot. It is said that there's only one thing worse than being a curate and that is having one. A facetious old saw but a partially truthful one. I know, for I was once a curate and remember how restless I became under the domination of a rector when I thought I knew as much as he did and believed I could perform many of the tasks of the ministry even better. A curate comes into a parish, much as a seminarian does, ready to learn, eager, maybe even humble. By the end of the first year he's learned the ropes, knows as much in the technical sense about the running of a parish as he needs to know, and is ready to fly high. Only his boss won't let him. The ministry has a way of encouraging the prima donna in us, and when the rector of a parish feels he's being upstaged by a young and able curate he usually doesn't like it. It makes him feel uncomfortable; it sometimes makes him damn sore.

This is only one aspect, though, to the relationship between rector and curate, which often is a warm, affectionate one that shows respect on both sides, and pride on the part of the rector in the growing accomplishments and confidence of his younger assistant.

My former curates have usually become good friends once they've gone on to their own parishes. This may in part be because they're relieved to be out from under my authority and on their own. But mostly because they understand when they're in charge themselves some of the dilemmas the rector himself must face. I like training men — seminarians and assistant ministers — but there will always be an element of competition between the "old man" and his protégé. Human nature doesn't change.

Usually, when the seminarians and I meet on Sunday mornings in my office, we talk about things that have occurred in the parish during the week that epitomize what parish life is like and what I've been up to. My hope is to elicit some kind of response. But often there's no visible reaction at all, since many of the things that I do have no meaning in their present lives.

Last Sunday, for instance, we talked about a young boy, the son of parishioners the seminarians knew, who is into heavy drugs. Randy, when I first knew him, was an attractive youngster who had just been kicked out of school for possessing marijuana and had come in to see me at the suggestion of his mother. Randy had everything going for him except his parents, who pushed him very hard. They were concerned to the point of making the youngster feel he was under constant scrutiny in order to accomplish, to succeed in a way which was probably beyond the reach of anyone his age. And so he turned to asocial behavior in school. This suggested to me that he was trying to get kicked out, so he could show his parents he couldn't measure up to what they expected of him.

Not surprisingly, I wasn't any help to him when he came to see me. He was polite but distant, friendly without in any way revealing what was really on his mind. One of the seminarians, Gerry, has gotten to know Randy in a casual way, and each Sunday he asks about him. Randy doesn't come to church any more, although his parents do, and it is through them that I keep in touch.

First pot. Then heavier stuff. Before long Randy, although still living at home, was seemingly lost to the straight world of his parents. Thin and withdrawn, the once bright and attractive boy seemed to have no place in his world for his family, for Gerry, or for me.

And then one day it happened. I didn't hear about it until Randy was in the psychiatric ward of Sibley Hospital, but when I did I wasn't really surprised. He'd tried to commit suicide by slashing his wrists one afternoon in his bedroom at home, and his mother found him, just in time. It seemed such a waste, this boy who would have graduated next June from high school and gone on to college, who had ability and intelligence and great charm.

Something had gone terribly wrong. What? His parents? Not entirely, for in spite of their overconcern for their son they were good people who in reality wanted good things for the boy they loved. Randy himself? You couldn't blame him for what was going on — for the pressures he was under from his parents and from a world in which he increasingly found himself a stranger.

The seminarians, with the exception of Gerry, were only theoretically interested in Randy. This was a dramatic experience that appealed to their love of crisis. But Randy was just too far removed from where the students are; their Sunday morning interests lay elsewhere in the realm of issues rather than in specific personalities. Whereas Gerry had been very quiet last week while we talked about Randy's family — about Randy's mother and father — about Randy himself. Gerry identified with Randy even though he only slightly knew him, and when Sunday morning was over Gerry asked if he could see me for a few minutes after church.

"I've been thinking a lot about Randy," he said. "Something's going on which I can understand. My father's always wanted me to succeed too and be like him, and one of the reasons I went to seminary, I think, was to please him. Maybe Randy and I have more in common than I'd realized. What do you say to my going to Sibley this afternoon and talking with him?"

Gerry did go over that afternoon, and three more times last week. Randy's still in the hospital and will probably be there for a while yet, but some kind of bond has been established between two young men, an eighteen-year-old boy who tried to take his life because he couldn't make it in his family and a twenty-three-year-old seminarian who's trying to make it in a more appropriate way, but who is also trying to discover who he is.

When I was in seminary at Cambridge I spent two years doing field work in a rundown church in South Boston. Along with the clinical training that I had during the summers in two hospitals, it was what got me through seminary and showed that I had some aptitude for the ministry. Grace Church in South Boston had had no resident minister for sixteen years, and for all that time it had been staffed by two seminarians each year who spent varying amounts of time at the church and in the community. My fellow seminarian and I discovered that the people were hungry for some attention. So besides putting in a full Sunday we spent two afternoons and evenings each week in the neighborhood of Grace Church. I organized a boys' club, using three students at Harvard whom I had taught in boarding school — appropriately a Catholic, a Protestant, and a Jew. The Catholic was on the track team at Harvard and the Jew on the wrestling team, while the Protestant was pious and nonathletic. But it didn't take much in the way of athletic or religious talents to gather a group of twelve-year-old boys in that part of the city; they were eager for something to do after school, and our two-day-a-week club became a success, more than the church services on Sunday. Another friend provided athletic equipment for us, and I gave what might have been called the inspiration. It worked for two years. But like a lot of well-meant philanthropic efforts the club never had any indigenous leadership, and it collapsed when I left Grace Church and my Harvard students graduated.

As a matter of fact, the church collapsed too. The Episcopal Diocese decided it wasn't worth pouring money into the operation of such a small congregation, just a handful of Welsh and Northern Irish Protestants who came there each week, some of them remembering the good old days when the four-hundred-seat Grace Church was almost filled on Sunday morning. We did well if we had thirty-five in the congregation.

But they were wonderful people and were especially kind to me. Mrs. Regan, who worked as a cleaning woman at Boston City Hospital, used to bring me homemade banana bread on Sunday morning which she'd baked on Saturday in her kerosene stove. The first time I tried it I was hungry enough to eat anything. The next week I took it to my fiancée's parents and discovered that the odor of kerosene had gone all the way from South Boston to the more privileged community of Wellesley. My future parents-in-law tactfully suggested I eat the bread in my room at the seminary and then come and visit Barbie.

Mrs. Regan was a saint, though, and banana bread was just one evidence of her diverse talents. She also played the piano in a bar in South Boston on Saturday night and the organ in Grace Church on Sunday morning. While the tunes were different, the style of the musician was the same. I shall never forget Mrs. Regan belting out "Onward, Christian Soldiers" or "Nearer, My God, To Thee." It made me want to go to her bar more than to her church. "Oh, Mr. Harper," Mrs. Regan told me one day, "I just love your sermons; they're the only time during the week

I can relax." That was a very high compliment indeed, because Mrs. Regan led a busy life, what with washing floors at the hospital, playing in the bar, baking banana bread, and being in church every time the door was open.

Even though I think St. John's is a good place for seminarians to learn about the ministry and that John Turnbull and I are reasonably good supervisors, seminarians miss something here which only an independent mission at a place like South Boston could give them. Today the seminaries require close, detailed supervision with innumerable conferences, in-depth interviews, and — perhaps — less initiative on the part of the student. This may be a good thing. I know I made a longer l'st of mistakes than any of the thirty-one men I've had in my parish ever thought of making. But in sp˙ e of my mistakes, I had opportunities in South Boston t at are denied most men who work in well-organized parishes like St. John's under supervision of p ople like myself and my clergy associates.

My mother once came to hear me p
Church. Instead of proudly admiring he   edgl'n
minister son, she sat through the entire   rvice with
her eyes tightly shut and with the most pained expression on her face. When the service was over I asked her how she'd liked it. Her reply was a faint smile and the briefest comment: "I hope you learn a lot here."

I did learn a lot. Once the Bishop of Massachusetts, who was known for his crustiness, came for a candlelight service which also happened to be Confirmation. I was proud of the three children and two adults I'd carefully prepared, but I wasn't ready for the quiz he proceeded to give them and me during the course of the service. I sat in a sweat of fear that my carefully trained students wouldn't measure up. I needn't have worried about them. They did just fine. I should have been worrying about myself. Because when the Bishop finished with the confirmation class, he took me on and proceeded in front of everyone to ask me complicated theological questions which only he (and possibly I) would understand. It was a kind of private joke, only I didn't see anything funny about it. I stumbled through the answers, and the Bishop finally got off my back and went on with the rest of the service in the candlelit church. But I got back at him in the sacristy later when, after he'd divested himself and was shaking hands at the coffee hour, I proceeded to fill his suitcase with candles. The next time the Bishop unpacked his bag, perhaps in some prestigious North Shore parish, he found twenty slightly burned candles in his luggage. I've learned since then to be a lot mo e respectful of bishops.

Grace Church used to have fine suppers. The Ir sh can eally put on a good feed when they put their minds and hands to it. Even though we had only a small congregation, each member had lots of relatives and friends, mostly Roman Catholics who were members of the neighboring St. Augustine's Parish. When Mrs. Northall and Mrs. Regan put together a church supper, the entire neighborhood turned out in the basement hall of the church. Banana bread was only a small part of the meal. I recall the time I held up one of Mrs. Northall's pies to show the assembled guests how great it was. One of the children who were forever running around knocked into me, and that was the end of Mrs. Northall's lemon meringue pie. It was almost the end of me.

People cried at Grace Church for a variety of reasons — hymns, sad sermons, Irish sentiment in general. My last Sunday there the church was awash in tears, mostly mine, for I was leaving — to graduate from seminary, to be ordained, and to get married, all in one week. It would be the last time I'd come to Grace Church, and the relationship that I'd managed to develop with people so delightfully open had come to an end. Old Mr. Northall, the Senior Warden, stood up and made a little speech; they presented me with a Bible inscribed and signed by the members of that small congregation; and we sang "Blest Be the Tie That Binds," accompanied by Mrs. Regan on the organ. Through my tears I could see her belting out the tune, the usual determined look on her face, and it seemed to me then (and after twenty years I think it's still true) that I could smell the banana bread that final Sunday at Grace Church in South Boston.

Last spring I sent a letter to the seminarians who've worked with me at St. John's, telling them about myself and about the parish. It was really an attempt to keep in touch with them and to let them know I was interested in what they were doing. For some of them the field work at St. John's was only a casual part of seminary training. For a few it was an unpleasant experience. Others found that their weekends on Lafayette Square provided good training for later years in the ministry.

This came out in some of the letters I received from these men in reply to mine. One said that what he's most learned was a degree of professionalism, of standards which the ministry often allows to go by the board. The dean of my own seminary used to say that the good clergyman should be the first man up on his block in the morning, by which he meant that the minister should work as hard as anyone else in his parish and to the extent that he is able keep disciplined hours. It is easy to stay in bed in the morning — except Sunday mornings — or take the afternoon off to play golf. No one but God will know.

Another former seminarian thanked me for taking him to task when he hadn't measured up to what I expected of him. He said he knew it had been a painful experience, as much for me as for him. I remember the occasion well and remember my anger as I told Bob that Sunday afternoon in my office that he didn't fulfill my idea of what a minister ought to be, that he'd better take a good look at himself. And yet it was Bob who that next summer sat up all night on the train from Edinburgh to London to be at Westminister Abbey when I was to preach. He knew what the occasion meant to me and he wanted to share in it with me. He had far more understanding of what it meant to be a pastor, or just plain friend, than I realized. I only half understood Bob that day I bawled him out in my office. I missed then the young man who later met me in London, and I came to see him more fully when seven years later he thanked me for the training he received at St. John's.

I wonder if he, and the others, realize the training they've given me, the support in a sometimes lonely job and the constant challenge to look at my own professionalism and my own standards, measured against some wise guys who as seminarians thought they had all the answers but who nonetheless cared about the same Christian ministry as I do.

Chapter 6

⸻

THE ELEVEN O'CLOCK service was a bust, as I knew it would be. I can't deal with too many problems at the same time, and this morning Linda and Michael were still very much on my mind. As I'd expected, they weren't in church for the service, and some of my tender feelings about them, especially about Michael, began to evaporate as I started to conduct a traditional Episcopal Service of Morning Prayer. They were there with me, however; they and people like them I've known who can't somehow plug into the formal religious expressions of public worship in church, yet who in their own way are as religious as most Sunday-after-Sunday churchgoing people. The professional part of me went right along with the liturgy at eleven o'clock, which after twenty years as a minister and a lot more before that as the son of one is second nature to me; the more personal me wondered how I was going to adapt the Marriage Service so that this couple and I would both be satisfied.

Then I suddenly thought of the policeman I'd seen on the way to church this morning. Don't ask me why he came to my mind as we were singing the words of the Venite: "O come, let us sing unto the Lord; let us heartily rejoice in the strength of our salvation." The policeman was a long way spiritually and probably physically from where I was at that moment, but he flashed through my mind and I could see him again as he went by me on Connecticut Avenue in his cruiser. At the time, something had told me that as a good cop he was aware of me and that so long as I obeyed the law and didn't behave in a bizarre manner he and I would never meet. It would only be when some crisis occurred that the cop and I would have a confrontation — if, say, I fell down on the sidewalk or threw a stone through one of the shop windows on Connecticut Avenue. Until the crisis came, if it ever did, we would remain strangers.

I can't say this all occurred to me in the exact way I'm telling it, but something like this did run through my mind, and I think I understand why. This was the way I met Linda and Michael. We were about to pass each other there in my office. Nothing was going to happen to any one of the three of us, because we didn't expect it to. I didn't expect them to engage me in any kind of serious relationship. I had figured out that the same was true for them. And then Michael precipitated a crisis by telling me he was Jewish and didn't buy our kind of marriage service. Then we met, the way the policeman and I haven't met yet, and the beginning of a relationship took place. That's probably overstating it, but as I looked over the congregation at the eleven o'clock service and thought of how fragile that kind of relationship is, how distant the congregation and I often are from each other, I realized that it is only when something dramatic, or at least a little out of the ordinary, happens that people get to know each other.

The service, as I say, wasn't very good. At least it wasn't very good for me. I remember years ago when I'd stayed up too late Saturday night and felt dreadful Sunday morning and could barely get through the eight o'clock Communion Service. A man took me aside afterwards and said he'd never been so moved by a service as by that one, that somehow I seemed more a part of it (more holy, did he mean?) than ever before.

So you see, you sometimes can go through the words and motions and not be there at all. Only I don't recommend it as a steady practice because sooner or later you'll get caught, the way I got caught the time I found myself saying the Lord's Prayer twice in the service. (Well, what's wrong with that, Mrs. Arlatt? After all, it was the prayer

Jesus taught us and you can't take that too lightly.) Or the time I started to celebrate Holy Communion, got halfway through the service, and finally realized there was no bread and wine on the altar. It doesn't take much to throw me off.

I like conducting public worship. I think I do it well. But my style isn't one that everyone likes. Because my understanding of holiness tends to be serious and even somber, that's the way worship is for me. I'm not much for a lot of joking and kidding around in church. I've had assistant ministers who're a lot more relaxed about these things than I am, and I envy them their ability to be so at ease, or to act in a way that is natural for them. I'm natural in church too, but that means that I like a more formal service.

St. John's is a strange church, although I doubt if anyone else would use that word and I do only because it's the first one that comes to mind. Let me explain. After all, conducting church services shouldn't be too much of a problem for most ministers; that's what we're in the business for, a lot of people think, and it's surprising to them when someone says that the conduct of public worship varies from church to church and minister to minister.

I've been Rector of St. John's for ten years, and I'm not used to my role yet. After I'd been here a year and was discouraged and homesick for the smaller, more homogeneous parish in Bedford that I'd left, I went to a friend who's known me for a long time and poured out my anxieties about my work to him. "Hell, John," he said, "the trouble with you is that up to now you've been in jobs that you're equal to. Now you're in one that's bigger than you and you can't get that through your head." He was right then, and it's still true. St. John's in many ways is bigger than I, even though by most standards I've done a better than average job in rebuilding a downtown parish.

People come here for all sorts of reasons. The most obvious — at least so it seems to me — is that it is a prestigious church, "The Church of the Presidents" on Lafayette Square in Washington, which boasts that every President of the United States from James Madison on has at one time or another attended services here. That's true, but it's hardly the President's church. The last President who was actually a member was Grover Cleveland, and that, in case you've forgotten, was a long time ago. But there is a lot of United States history connected with St. John's. Over the years since it was built in 1815 many of the leaders in our country's history have worshipped here. So, I suppose, people come here hoping to see the great of the present, or get a whiff of the ghosts of the past.

St. John's was once a "society" church, as well as an historic one, and I can't help look around the congregation and wonder sometimes if that's the reason Mrs. A. comes here or Colonel B., and whether this is the only reason people like the C's still make any pretense of remaining members of the parish. Is it important in the society column or an obituary to note that so-and-so is or was a member of St. John's on Lafayette Square? For some people it is. That's one of the reasons some of them are in church this morning — to be sure their credentials are right when they marry and when they die.

But there are other reasons, better ones I think, why people come here. They have to do with the vitality of this old church, with the excellence of the music and the Sunday School, and maybe with the preaching.

I'm conscious of this last reason because I'm mostly responsible for the sermons at St. John's. Now I'm under no illusions about being a great preacher. I know I'm not. What I am, most of the time, is honest. While some of the more traditional members of the flock have occasionally been dismayed, and some of them have actually left, there are others who come here because they expect to hear a fifteen-minute sermon in which the preacher shares his own doubts as well as his certainties. The process of sharing isn't always clear nor is the means as good as it might be: those are two reasons I'm not the greatest preacher in the world. What I do attempt to get across is an interpretation of Christianity which is acceptable to me and at least mostly acceptable to some other searching people also.

I don't have many answers. My own life is filled with contradictions and indeed with what is often called sin, and which I also think of as ambiguity and alienation, a mixture of things good and bad. Occasionally I'm courageous enough to talk about these things on Sunday morning, not specifically using myself as an example, but at least talking out of my own experience and with some understanding of the experience of the people in the pews.

There are those who don't like this kind of preaching; proclamation rather than the search for faith is more their cup of tea. I can only say that over the last ten years there have been people who have found St. John's a congenial place in which to ask questions and look for possible solutions to their lives. Sometimes they have found the solutions in the traditional formula of religion, sometimes in quite unexpected, unorthodox ways. I myself have found certainty in both approaches, and I would like to encourage the congregation to do likewise.

The people before me in this strange church, therefore, are a mixture of expectations. It is also true that some have no real expectations at all, like Mrs. Mason, who's been attending St. John's for seventy years, never listens to the sermon or pays attention to the words of the hymns or to what contemporary translations of the Bible say about her life. She basks in the warm glow of Sunday worship and is simply glad to be here today away from the storms of her own and her family's lives. That's all she asks of religion, to be warmed for a little while and not to be any more upset or involved than she already is. There are others in the congregation who feel as she does.

"O God, help us to become masters of ourselves that we may become the servants of others.

Take our lips and speak through them;
Take our minds and think through them;
And take our hearts and set them on fire."

Not everyone is ready for a challenge this morning; not all the worshippers want their consciences pricked or, as the prayer says, their "hearts set on fire." They want to be warmed, but by a different kind of fire than the one I sometimes have in mind when I use that prayer at the beginning of a sermon to say to others and to myself what Christianity should try to do.

St. John's is a graceful building, and that's one of its strengths — and one of its weaknesses. When it was built in 1815 by Benjamin Henry Latrobe, the great architect who introduced the Greek revival style to this country, he wrote to a friend that he had just designed a church in Washington "which will make many Washingtonians religious who have not been religious before." I suppose the building has done that for some people over the years, for it is a lovely building — President Kennedy referred to it one day as "the little yellow church across the Square" — and while inside it is now a mishmash of different tastes and periods, it is still one of Latrobe's masterpieces. The windows and pews are late nineteenth century, the marble columns at the side of the chancel and the east wall were installed by Renwick, and the furnishings in the chancel are of a later period.

Taken together, St. John's is a gem of a building,

simple and thoroughly American. Its style belongs to a new country and to a new capital which had just been founded on the banks of the Potomac River. Granted, it finds itself physically dwarfed by the headquarters of the AFL-CIO and the Veterans Administration. Granted, it looks across to the President's House (which Latrobe also had a hand in restoring after the War of 1812). Granted, it stands "on the greatest square in the greatest city in the world." Nevertheless, it seems to proclaim that institutional religion cannot be overshadowed by what is secular. St. John's has its place in the scheme of things.

Many people have been drawn to St. John's instinctively and not always in a way that they can articulate. The quiet beauty of a relatively small church set amid the symbols of American power has been a compelling reason why people drive a half hour or more to be in church on Sunday morning, or why they take part in a parish program which can never hope to resemble the community of individual men and women which the Church at its best would like to be.

When Lincoln attended St. John's the Sunday before his inauguration he was unrecognized by the rector until halfway through the service, which has always seemed to me a fair division of the respect of church and state. When Lyndon Johnson used to come here he preferred to slip in quietly, much to our chagrin. Never, so far as I remember, did he sit in the official President's Pew, but rather in a variety of places within the church. John Kennedy and I were both in the Spee Club at Harvard, and I first met him in 1946 when he ran for Congress. As a matter of fact, he once gave me his skis, which are still a proud possession. President Kennedy came to St. John's in March, 1963, when I was instituted as the thirteenth rector of the parish. I suddenly realized as I addressed him at the foot of the chancel steps where he had gone to sign our Presidential Prayer Book that I, a boy from Winthrop, Massachusetts, was addressing the President of the United States.

But why not? We are rightly awed by our institutions, that of the Presidency, to name one. The life of the nation depends on respect for these institutions and the men and women who serve them. But the Church, which is only one institution among many in this society, has a clear right to speak out on matters that affect the lives of men and women.

When I was asked to become Rector of St. John's, I told the Vestry that I didn't think my preaching was exactly what a post like St. John's needed.

"What you should have," I said, "is a prophetic preacher, like one of the Old Testament prophets; someone who will make the headlines of the Washington *Post* on Monday morning, who will be both courageous and controversial. That's not my style," I added, "even though there are times I wish it were."

The members of the Vestry quickly assured me, almost in unison, that this was precisely the kind of preacher they didn't want. They didn't want religion, they said, to get mixed up in the affairs of the White House, the AFL-CIO, or any of the other secular institutions in American society.

For ten years now we have battled over this issue, because there are other people at St. John's who fervently believe that religion has an obligation to speak out on all issues involving human lives. When Barbie in 1965 walked in a picket line in front of the White House protesting the treatment of Negroes in Selma, Alabama, some of the parishioners thought the world had come to an end. I've not been nearly as courageous as I'd like to have been; I've sometimes equivocated about my relationship to a diverse parish, knowing the need to keep open lines of communications with all sides. However, as a parish we have supported some of the protests that have taken place in Washington over the last years, especially those having to do with race and the war in Vietnam. But St. John's trumpet has not been as loud as I might now in retrospect wish it had been.

President Nixon holds occasional Sunday worship services in the White House, and I suspected that in the course of time I'd be asked to officiate at one. What should I do? I mistrust those services which seem to merge the institutions of religion and the state, which downgrade the plurality of denominational worship and which make religion an even more exclusive experience than it already is for many people. I received a call from the White House inviting me to preach there on Sunday, May 9, 1971 —

"Mother's Day Sunday," I was told by the White House aide who called me. Instead of accepting or declining (I really think I was ready to say I wouldn't come) I called three of my friends, all Democrats, to ask their advice. One, an architect, said that if he were asked by the President to design something for the White House which would be beneath his professional dignity, he would still accept the commission because he had been asked by the President of the United States. The second and third people I asked were both clergymen and both urged me to accept.

"How many times have you given prayers at conventions and businessmen's banquets even when you've not been in sympathy with the group you're addressing?" my friend Bob Estill asked. "How often have you married couples who you know are only using the church for social reasons? Yet you do marry them, don't you?"

I called the White House and accepted, and wrote a careful sermon about the place of hope in human life. My clergyman brother was incensed by what I didn't say. "You had a golden opportunity," Ralph wrote me, "to address the President on the issue of the war, which is the main issue in our country today, and were too much of a coward to do your job. The Old Testament prophets would have spoken up; but you were afraid to."

In the largest sense, my brother was obviously right, and that's what's wrong with the White House services. But I don't feel a man's home is the place to argue with him, whether it's a worship service or a cocktail party. Something inside me recoils from publicly chastising another person, particularly when he's asked me to be a guest in his house. Preaching at the White House does indeed inhibit what one says. Yet I would probably have preached that same sermon to the President in St. John's, because the meaning of a "reasonable hope" was on my mind just then. In fact, I might not have given the kind of disturbing, challenging words that Ralph wanted me to give at any time or any place.

That's the bind the preacher is always in as he prepares a sermon and thinks about the people to whom he is to speak. Does he say what's on his mind and let the chips fall where they may? Does he tailor his message to his listeners in the belief that they will more readily listen to him if he speaks a language they can understand? To what extent does the preacher reenact the prophetic role of Israel's great men and to what extent is he himself, a human being, wanting to be heard by all elements of his congregation?

As I say, I think I would have talked about hope in any event that Sunday, whether at the White House or in some less difficult setting. But there are other times when I have been less certain. Looking at the people in the pews, some of whom I know intimately, I wonder about this religious search that I want to make with them. If it's the blind leading the blind, it's no good. If the one-eyed man is too far out front, the blind will fall away and the one-eyed leader's own limited vision will possibly cause him to stumble. I wish I were always sure how the search can best be made and where it will lead.

The only kind of religion that I understand is the struggle that people make together. My brother Ralph's view of the Church and its preachers is that of authority speaking out so that those below, including the President, get the word. Strangely enough, some of my conservative friends would agree with him, though not when it comes to telling the country what to do. They would have the priest speak with the authority of his office and not allow his doubts or his humanity to show through. They want to hear the Word of God as it is contained for them in the Bible and in tradition. They want religion clear-cut, decisive, final.

When Dag Hammarskjold's diary, *Markings*, was first published it made a big impression on me. I talked about it in a lot of sermons. Here, it seemed to me, was the contemporary religious man at his best. The inner struggle of the Secretary General of the United Nations was revealed underneath the facade of a highly successful diplomat; the religious man and the man who functioned effectively in his work were indeed the same. While it must not have been easy for Hammarskjold, it was possible for him to hold both sides in some sort of creative tension. He had some of the answers, but not all of them; he was cautious about himself in those areas where he could afford to indulge his introspection and bold in those other, public parts of his life where decisions had to be quickly made and actions performed with courage. He would have been a disappointment, as indeed he was to some, to many of the traditionally inclined church people who are embarrassed when their leaders don't provide the answers they think they are looking for on Sunday morning, and when they purposely permit religion to be unstructured.

Hammarskjold's religion, it seems to me, *was* unstructured, but it was perhaps a more honest faith than much of what passes for religion among many of my friends. Ralph and others at one end of the religious spectrum want the Church to be uncompromising; I don't see it that way, either for the Church or for myself.

And this has led me, as the service ends this morning, to think once more about a marriage which in a few days I'll be performing, where the name of Jesus will be omitted, where a liturgy which has meant much to so many will be butchered and made to sound less beautiful, and where two people will commit themselves publicly to each other in what, after all, is a rather fortuitous relationship. I don't ask them to accept the Apostles' Creed or come to Holy Communion or even be baptized Christians, just as I don't examine too closely all the motives of why people are at St. John's today. Instead, I ask them to be honest about each other, their intentions toward one another.

In asking this of Linda and Michael I am also asking something of myself.

Chapter 7

To STAND AT THE DOOR of the church after a service is one of the hardest things a minister has to do. At least I find it hard. I've had my mind on one thing, conducting a church service, while the several hundred people who file past me coming out the door have several hundred different things on their minds, all of them important to them. A minister is a little like an actor in that he's been onstage, doing his bit for the Lord, but where an actor retires to his dressing room backstage when the play's over, the minister heads for the lobby, as it were, and shakes the hand of each "customer."

It's important to have this personal contact with parishioners and visitors, and for them to feel they have some relationship to the rector. But it's hard going. My body's arm reaches out for the first hand that's offered, and for the next fifteen minutes the narrow aisles of St. John's Church will empty a variety of people out to the front door, where I'll be waiting to greet them. Many of them will be impatient to get home; others will want to stand and chat.

"I'm new in Washington," says a visitor who is first out the door, "and I did so enjoy your service."

"Why didn't you use the General Thanksgiving today?" demands a second.

"Please don't forget to send me a copy of last year's Easter sermon; I liked that part about . . ."

"Young man, you're nice to welcome me, but I've been a member of this parish for sixty-three years, only I don't get to church very often. My grandmother . . ."

"Gee, John, when are we going to get together for lunch? You free on Thursday?"

So it goes, or rather so the first people out the door go. I try to remember the name of the newcomer to Washington so I can call on him this week; I'll try not to forget the General Thanksgiving next Sunday; I'll have to find a copy somewhere of the Easter sermon; I'll do my best to recognize old Mrs. Campbell when she next comes to church; and I'll put my ring on my other hand so I won't forget lunch with Phil Watts on Thursday; that is, if I haven't already made another date and if my ring's not already on the wrong finger.

I glance toward the door from which people are coming to see who might be next. My former Senior Warden and good friend, Phil Watts, is a happy interlude in the line, and lunch with him will be a pleasant diversion this week. But there's a different kind of diversion coming along next in the person of Miss Lydia Morris Morrison, fifth-generation member of the parish and one-thousandth-generation Christian — a professional one at that, who knows more about early Church heresies than I ever dreamed of and is perfectly capable of finding heresies in the present day as well. She'd make a good Bishop. Like the fundamentalist preacher who claimed, "I can smell sin," Miss Lydia Morris Morrison can smell heresies of every kind, and she is forthright enough to take out her sword when she does. Unlike most reformers, though, she has a sense of humor.

While we violently disagree about a number of things, I enjoy her, except when she comes through the line after church on Sunday and wants to tell me of her newest discoveries of heretical leanings, of the letters she's written to Bishop Creighton, and of the response the poor beleaguered man made to her latest attack. Bishops must be even more patient than parish ministers, and Miss Morrison's typewriter must need a new ribbon almost every month for all the letters she writes.

One of the reasons she types is that many of her letters are sent anonymously. She revels in her subterfuges, and for a long time I've had a suspicion that she enjoys the possibility of being found out.

Last month a clergyman friend of mine who's more conservative than I am wrote a letter to our diocesan newspaper bemoaning the fate of the Book of Common Prayer, how it was being superseded by newer liturgies and how much of the grandeur of sixteenth-century language is lost today in the Episcopal Church. He believes this and is quite sincere in his defense of the past, which he feels is unnecessarily being forgotten in favor of what he likes to call "modernity." Miss Morrison obviously agrees. On reading my friend Clem's letter she proceeded to send Clem one of her anonymous missives. Because she identified herself as being a long-time member of St. John's, Clem showed me the letter. The typing and the manner of expression were a dead giveaway.

Miss Morrison's letter to Clem read as follows:

Dear Mr. Stone,

This is an anonymous but fervent thank you for your straight-from-the-shoulder letter of protest in the last issue of the 'Washington Diocese'. You express my feelings exactly and indeed over the past years have done so both to the Bishop and to the Church at large. I do not refer, of course to the Larger Church, for that would include the saints in heaven, but I think you know what I mean. These heretical tendencies must be rooted out through the vigilance, courage, and action of people like ourselves.

I've cut out your fine letter and mailed it (also anonymously) to my rector in case he hasn't seen it. I doubt if he reads as many church periodicals as I do. He's young and very starry-eyed, and although this parish is full of aged die-hards like me, he is trying to placate everybody, with garbled versions of liturgies; and the result is rather a mess, poor man. I think you know the tendencies today of some of the newer clergy, especially those who have graduated from the seminary in Cambridge, and were I not firmly established after many years at St. John's I would consider transferring to your parish.

Have you considered hammering home your crusade with a frequent bombardment of protests signed with various nom-de-plumes? That would be in a good cause for the Lord of Hosts. I shall be watching.

"Lydia, what have you been up to now?" I laughingly greeted her at the door of St. John's. "I understand you've been writing my friend Clem Stone. You'd better watch those letters to younger clergy. Maybe Clem will take you seriously."

"But — but —" she stuttered, "how did you find out?" And then she broke into the smile of a person who's been caught in the course of a good

95

crusade. "It was a good letter, don't you think, John? You know I'm right, only you won't admit it. Someday somebody will listen to me."

I could see that Miss Lydia Morris Morrison was being pushed from behind by people in the line who wanted to shake the minister's hand, too, and get home for lunch — people who weren't interested in a conversation between the rector and an elderly lady with a walking stick which she waved like a fairy godmother trying to turn a reluctant frog into an unlikely prince. (The only way I'll become a prince in Miss Lydia Morris Morrison's eyes will be to renounce "the hidden works of darkness," and that will mean joining her crusade for the preservation of the Book of Common Prayer.)

Lydia held her ground. "John, why don't *you* write anonymous letters to the *Washington Diocese*? That way, my cause gets served and you can have fun too. No one need know, just you and me."

"I'll think about it, Lydia," I answered. I was even tempted to tell her that I approve of her Society for the Preservation of the Book of Common Prayer. For it's a book I love, too, and it's been at the heart of my devotions for as long as I can remember.

But no, Miss Morrison, not on your life. Go on now and try to interest someone else in your crusade; I'm not for sale, at least not this morning at the end of the eleven o'clock service.

Get someone else to help you bombard the newspapers, because next Sunday we're going to have a jazz mass at St. John's, with bearded players, folk music, guitars, and God-knows-what-else. You'll have warning in the weekly parish *Leaflet* if you don't want to come, but you'll be there, I know, because you always come to church and unless it's different from the last time, you'll be moved despite yourself and you'll be glad you came. And anyway, how could you complain to your friends on Monday about Sunday's shenanigans if you hadn't even been there yourself?

We won't do this often, Miss Morrison, so don't worry. The week after next it'll be back to the Prayer Book and Bach and the deep-throated organ, and you'll feel like you're in church again the way you've always known church and the way you expect always to know it.

Miss Morrison is followed by the small plump figure of Mrs. Headley, whose still-beautiful face gives no indication of the pain within. I have been privy to Mrs. Headley's problems ever since I first came to St. John's and neither she nor I nor her doctor know any ultimate solution to the wrecked life of her divorced daughter Jenny. It was Jenny herself who came to see me soon after I arrived in Washington. A once-beautiful woman now in her early fifties, she was briefly married to a very rich and prominent Washingtonian who eventually left her for another woman. That was when Jenny's drinking began. Disgraced and lonely for companionship, she moved into her mother's lovely home in Georgetown and for a while, she told me, it looked as though the widowed mother and the divorced daughter could live together in some kind of harmony.

Mrs. Headley, for all her breeding and social graces, isn't an easy person to live with. She's demanding of people around her, in her own way she's spoiled and selfish, and having Jenny at hand has only increased her possessiveness, not to mention her desire to make her daughter into a person Jenny certainly is not. For Jenny is carefree and has no interest in good works. She prefers TV serials to serious books, people younger than herself to the conservative friends her mother entertains at home. In short, Jenny, who is dependent on her mother now, is a rebel; alcohol has become one way by which she can show her mother that she wants to live her own life.

But booze is killing Jenny and she knows it. That's what she came to see me about, in spite of the fact that ostensibly it was to see if I could help her find a way out of her mother's clutches. Jenny admitted that day, almost ten years ago, that she drinks too much (she's never said she was an alcoholic, at least not to me), and as I've watched her over the years I've seen an attractive woman die gradually before my eyes. Jenny, in fact, spends her entire day in the company of the bottle, which she hides where her prying mother can't find it. She is always slightly tight and lives constantly with a low-grade hangover. Her good looks are gone, people find it difficult to have her at their parties, and gradually she's retreated into a world which includes fewer and fewer people (among them her mother, and the maid who adores her, and, I suppose, myself).

I'm a paradox in Jenny's life. She never comes to church, because her mother's always there and she says she herself isn't interested in religion. Yet I know I'm one of the few anchors in Jenny's life, and I try to visit her when her mother isn't home, and I talk to her whenever she calls me — usually late at night when she's lonely and often very drunk.

Even though I'm angry with her for what she's making of her life, I can't give up on Jenny. I care about her. I care that her mother won't give her the means to live on her own and get the professional help she needs. Mrs. Headley is against psychiatrists, Alcoholics Anonymous, any sort of assistance that might come to grips with her daughter's problems. She tells me that Jenny is a "little indisposed," that she will soon be all right again. We carry on this little charade, Mrs. Headley and I, when we greet each other on Sunday morning after we've finished saying our prayers in a service which tries to help people be honest.

Has Mrs. Headley been talking to God this morning in church about Jenny's sickness and about her own failure, or has she tried to fool God the way she tries to fool herself and me? Mrs. Headley, so beautifully dressed this morning to greet her Maker, will return from church to greet her hungover daughter, who will just be getting out of bed with two drinks already inside her. Together they will have a "little sherry" in the darkened library of the Headley townhouse while both women suffer inside and have no way of telling each other about their pain. They will lie to each other, as Mrs. Headley has perhaps lied this morning to God and certainly as Jenny has been lying to herself, and Jenny will continue to drink and try to shut out the reminders of her sorrows.

I don't know whom I am sorrier for. But I want, as I stand here at the door of the church, to be God for both these people and to enter, perhaps unbidden, into their lives and change them into something good. It's not going to happen that way, I know, and yet I keep trying, trying to reach Jenny in a way that will help her and looking for the means, perhaps through the church service, of also reaching her mother so that she will wake up before that final end comes and it's all too late.

"Why does mother keep at me?" Jenny once said to me. Remembering that question now I recall another that Mrs. Headley put to me, "Why won't Jenny love me more?"

I don't know! I don't know! I want to yell at them both. I don't know why two perfectly nice women are at each other's throats all the time, why one is drinking herself to death and the other longs to die in a different way, both to avoid the hurt which they feel inside. I don't know why these things happen, but I know both these women are real and what each says about the other is partly true. I don't know why people won't love one another, especially where there is such longing on each side for approval and acceptance.

Mrs. Headley comes each Sunday to church in the belief that God will set everything right, much as some of Jenny's friends go to psychiatrists in the belief that a doctor can make them well without their doing anything on their own. Religion and psychiatry don't mean a thing until you become a believer, and a believer is someone who acts rather than who waits for everything to fall into place. A believer is an active, rather than a passive, person, for he knows that spiritual and physical health are a cooperative process and that God can only work within human experience when people let Him. Mrs. Headley on her knees is only half a person; Mrs. Headley at home with Jenny is the other half. Jenny and her bottle are only part of the real Jenny, who once could look at herself in a different way, and perhaps can do so again if she really wants to.

Peppery Miss Morrison and the distraught Mrs. Headley are two of the people I care about on Sunday morning, although I'll probably never be the priest Lydia Morrison wants nor the pastor Mrs. Headley needs. Nor the preacher young Stuart Moody looks for when he comes to church. Stu is a graduate student at George Washington University, which is several blocks from St. John's, and I noticed him in the early fall in the side balcony at the eleven o'clock service. We don't have that many younger

people in the congregation. The few we have stand
out. When I finally put a name to his face and
learned a little about him, he asked if he could come
in to talk with me. His problem was simple he said:
he'd stopped believing in God.

Well, he'd come to the right man all right!

Stu was born in the Middle West and came from a
very conservative religious background. He'd always gone to church and been active in its activities, and after graduating from a small fundamentalist college in Ohio he found his way to G. W. and
graduate school. Washington, big-city life, the East,
the variety of students at G. W. — they all confused
Stu. Living in a graduate dormitory didn't help
either.

It was about this time that he found his way to
St. John's, which he said he liked even though the
service is utterly different from anything he's known
before.

I am different too, he admits. He says preachers at
home never deal with controversial social issues, and
he's not quite sure preachers should. They're good
men, he tells me, who talk a lot about the Bible and
Jesus and about being good. But goodness, he says, is
perhaps easier in a small Midwestern town than it is
in Washington, the Bible easier to expound when
evidences of power aren't all around or slums or
black people or poor people. It's easier in Stu's home-
town to be a practicing Christian, he feels, than it is
in a G. W. dorm or even at St. John's Church. Although I disagree with him, I know what he means:

college was a spiritually disrupting experience for me, too, and it was only after the Navy and teaching that I found myself on firm ground again.

Stu wants to talk about his faltering faith with someone who will share his trouble with him; he's genuine in his concern for whatever it is he feels he's lost. Not God really, but the comfortable assurances he once had about God. He's going to have to go through a period of reassessment and maybe readjustment as well. He's not lost his faith, I tell him; it's only taking a new and probably more exciting turn.

And so I smile at Stu this morning and ask how it's going with him. I'm glad he's in church along with Mrs. Headley; she needs to know a seeker like Stu, someone who's looking for answers to his questions. She needs to know, as does Miss Morrison, someone who doubts and then finds his way home again and who wants to share the discovery with someone else.

Chapter 8

WHEN I BECAME RECTOR of St. Matthew's Church in Bedford, New York, the Vestry said not to worry about money, mine or the parish's. "We'll take care of that," Bartow Farr, the Senior Warden, told me. And they did. In the time I was there I never had to concern myself about where the next dollar for the church was coming from. In previous years the deficit had been annually made up on the club car between Mt. Kisco and Grand Central. (When Jack Livingstone, one of the Vestrymen, said, "It's your turn, Lewie, to fill the gap this year," what Jack meant was that Lewis Anderson, a rich New York banker, would come up with five or ten thousand dollars either from his own or his friends' pockets, and St. Matthew's would be solvent for another twelve months.) The Vestry was also generous in taking care of its rector. The thoughtful Senior Warden kept the rectory "cellar" well stocked and the practical banker-treasurer made sure that the minister's other needs were looked after. We were very fortunate, and we knew it. Bartow Farr and Lee Brown were not only good friends but concerned ones as well.

But after a few years in that blissful state it began to occur to me that, however kindly, I was being seduced, not so much by people as by an attitude. Money's not a dirty word, I thought to myself one day when I began to question the unspoken parish policy of never discussing money from the pulpit. After all, most of my flock spent five days a week making large basketfuls of the stuff and finding ways of spending it, and many of them were exceedingly moral people. Why shouldn't the church likewise be concerned, and publicly so, with getting and giving? Men who worked on Wall Street might have enough of finances during the working week but that was no reason why I couldn't get my ideas in about money on Sunday from the pulpit.

I left St. Matthew's before I got around to working out just how the whole subject of stewardship could be tackled in that affluent parish, and to this day I don't know exactly what I would have done. St. Matthew's really didn't need large amounts of money. It was adequately taken care of, not just by the Lewie Andersons and the Mrs. Stantons of the parish, but increasingly by other, younger, parishioners.

Even if I were sufficiently eloquent to persuade people to give more to the church, I wonder whether the parish might have been any wiser in its use of income than many philanthropic institutions are. The lovely forty acres of St. Matthew's charming churchyard seemed to be cared for well enough on a modest budget. As it was, the Rector's salary, sufficient to keep him from being the poorest man in town, would have been the envy of many of my colleagues in the ministry. Money wasn't a dirty word in Bedford; it just wasn't the most important one for their parish in the eyes of a lot of people. More spiritual concerns, I was subtly told, should be on the agenda. The ways a man earned his living and spent it were not the main focus of religion. The Church should be about other things, my friends said.

Perhaps if the parish in those days had been more involved with the diocese and the national offices of the Episcopal Church, we might have found the imperative to raise money through St. Matthew's well-heeled parishioners for work in places other than Bedford. To some extent we did begin to do this, though in a small way compared to the potential resources. I believe my successor has had better luck in this regard than I; perhaps the parish itself has changed.

I seriously question why any local church should raise more for its own needs than is required for simple, basic maintenance and for paying salaries. I know this is sometimes hard to get across to people, because their first loyalty is usually to their own parish and only begrudgingly to the wider church, diocese, or national "headquarters." The national church often seems remote from local needs, and is frequently to the left of the local parish position, both politically and theologically.

Indeed, the Episcopal Church and its national leaders have in recent years been notably forthright in championing programs for social change. I am proud of this. The Church has tried to relate its potential for leadership to the needs of the times. Parishes like Bedford can be of enormous help if vestries are willing to turn over some of their income and are themselves willing, as some of Bedford's people are, to serve on national or diocesan committees.

But I don't blame a person for contributing only a token amount to the parish when he recognizes that it really doesn't need more money in order to maintain its own parochial programs, to heat and paint the church, to pay the Rector's salary. And I'm sympathetic with those whose financial loyalty is first to the parish which, after all, is the visible evidence of the Christian institution. When Lewie Anderson and Mrs. Stanton give their annual check to St. Matthew's or St. Swithin's they are supporting what they love, and until someone can convince them of an important need elsewhere, that lawns and beautiful buildings are not all there is to the

Gospel, I don't suppose they will ever be willing to do more than they now do.

Mrs. Stanton and I have a lot in common. Reluctantly, I have to confess that my first loyalty is usually to what I can see and touch — and in the case of the church, smell. I have to stretch my Christian commitment to give sacrificially to what I know is important but which doesn't affect my own life directly. I'm not so different from others who need to be educated in the basic concept of giving without strings attached or without a personal return on the investment.

Washington is, of course, a very different place from Bedford, even if St. John's and St. Matthew's share many common problems. The main difference is that St. John's has more people and more money, including a hefty endowment (which in my judgment is a good thing for a city church, if it uses the income to maintain a ministry to the city). Because St. John's is a more varied parish in its membership than St. Matthew's it has less wealth per capita, but because of the generosity of the past it has a yearly budget of well over three hundred and fifty thousand dollars.

Most of this, I am glad to say, is raised from the living. The problem is that the living will soon be dead. The generous parishioners tend to be older people, and one wonders who will replace them. My generation (the younger crowd) either won't have large amounts of inherited wealth, which is where some of our income now comes from, or else — and this is more serious — my generation and the one coming on its heels may simply not care about the Church one way or another. If the Church becomes irrelevant to society, if it permits its clergy and lay leadership to hide from more worldly issues, if it becomes a museum of supposed past glories, then people will put their money into other agencies of society which will seem more viable to them.

We have recently had two highly successful money-raising programs at St. John's. In both instances we have asked people to make a pledge to the work of the church (much of the money going outside the parish into our own outreach programs and diocesan missionary efforts) on a three-year basis. We have raised a total amount in excess of a million and a half dollars, and I have to admit my pleasure in taking part in these two campaigns.

It will, as I say, get harder to raise money if membership in American churches declines. But I strongly believe that a church like St. John's, with its tremendous potential for leadership in the urban community, can make wise use of as much money as people will give. If we are bold enough to talk honestly and with complete candor, people will listen to what we have to say and, as has been proven twice in Washington, they will also give generously both to their own parish's programs and to those which are, strictly speaking, outside the local church's domain. The day-care center, the psychiatric counseling service, the community social center, the ghetto housing program, the various inner-city programs — all of these St. John's today supports not only with its members' money, but in many instances through its members' personal involvement as well.

Every fall when the Vestry plans the budget for the coming year there is careful and sometimes heated discussion about priorities. The security and maintenance of our valuable, historic buildings is a recurring subject. Because we are downtown, we constantly have to deal with vandalism and theft. In the past two years we have lost three candlesticks, ten microphones, one Bible, and two typewriters. The "poorbox" in the Narthex has been rifled on five occasions. The lectern which holds the Bible has been turned over and damaged, eggs have been thrown at the cross on the altar, cushions in pews have been destroyed, and last summer, for the third time in my ten years' rectorate, the church was set on fire and was miraculously saved by the prompt action of the fire department. All of this in order to keep the church open from seven A.M. until the offices close late in the afternoon.

Is it worth it? The Vestry has answered with a resounding "Yes," even though they and I are well aware of our stewardship (another use for that word) of historic buildings. We want this to be a "church for all people," and unfortunately we recognize that "all" encompasses a wide variety of the well and the sick. Fire and burglar systems, guards, volunteers at the door to greet (and surreptitiously watch) people during the week, and surveillance by the staff can help to reduce the danger, but as long as we mean what we say about wanting St. John's to be a useful instrument in the human religious quest, then we will continue to run serious risks and ones which sometimes cause us a great deal of worry.

Demonstrations in front of the White House on Lafayette Square, danger on the streets and in the Square itself at night, vandalism and robbery are very real threats to St. John's. Yet in another sense they are part and parcel of our religious, or theological, concern. The church does not exist merely for its own members but for those outside its walls; it is a vehicle for telling men and women about God and our relationship to Him. Its physical walls, the stained glass windows, candlesticks, and needlepoint cushions may help to tell the message better to some people, but they are not the message. The message can be told when the cherry blossoms are on the trees and Lafayette Park is at its most beautiful and when people look at St. John's yellow walls and admire its beauty. And the message can also be told when angry citizens crowd the streets, when they engage in behavior that is disruptive and even unlawful, when the beauty of Latrobe's building is blurred by tear gas and surrounded with obscenities. The building is not the message. The Gospel message is spoken more through people than through things, and more through actions than through words — no matter how beautifully articulated and hallowed the words are by centuries of use.

Nevertheless, people still enter St. John's and give money to it because it is a symbol to them of the message. Somewhere between fifty and a hundred people come into the church each day to sit quietly within "the sound of gentle stillness." Because we are constantly exposed to damage or theft, we will have trouble in succeeding years getting adequate insurance coverage for such a building and for the handsome nineteenth-century Parish House which adjoins the church and which was the former British Legation headquarters.

The offerings which people make when the plate is passed or when they make an annual gift or put money in the almsbox may become less; we may not be able to afford the luxury of painting inside and out as often as we have been doing; nor spend annually over thirty thousand dollars for superb music and a gifted organist.

Three clergy are paid well, given comfortable homes in which to live, travel allowances and other perquisites; a total staff of fourteen men and women receive from the parish incomes in line with other salaries in Washington: all these may have to be modified if church-going in the United States declines. I would like to see our endowment grow to three or four million dollars, so that we can be sure of maintaining those aspects of our ministry to the city and diocese that the Vestry feels are important.

The annual budget at St. John's has more than doubled in ten years. While the principal of the endowment has not grown substantially, the giving on the part of our members has. (Money for many is not a dirty word, after all.) But the large part of the money comes, as I indicated, from older, devoted parishioners. They have given generously for maintenance and for other kinds of material improvement; they are willing to support the clergy financially and to be sure that the staff is well compensated; and when challenged with new programs and outreach into the community, most of St. John's members have some vision of what the church means beyond our own boundaries.

Not everyone, to be sure, cares much about the Diocese, the Bishop, the national Church; not everyone at St. John's has much interest in how our investments are made or about the companies in which we hold stocks; and not everyone wants to see the Church in the 1970's on the cutting edge of social or political issues.

Others feel differently, thank God, and the really amazing thing about this parish is that in spite of various fires of discontent with parochial and national Church programs, St. John's people have been remarkably resilient, open-minded, and generous. As a matter of fact, for what is often considered a conservative, stuffy old parish we are surprisingly relevant and even — perish the thought — sometimes quite liberal.

At this point I ought to say something about how I got to St. John's, or rather why I work on Lafayette Square in Washington and not, say, in a ghetto church or in some less comfortable post. I didn't plan it this way. I'm probably as ambitious as the next man, but neither the job at St. Matthew's nor at St. John's came about because I wanted to be rector of either of those parishes. I didn't. The choice, to be sure, was ultimately mine, but the invitation (or "call," as we say in the trade) came unexpectedly. In both cases I resisted accepting.

Let me explain. When I went to seminary I was unsure about going into the ministry at all. I was tired of teaching *Silas Marner* and *A Tale of Two Cities* to bored schoolboys. I wasn't a very good and certainly not a very exciting nor imaginative teacher. After four years in a boarding school I began to sense there was more to life than I was then experiencing. I went to seminary in Cambridge, Massachusetts, with the vague idea of spending a year in graduate study and then of reevaluating my place as a teacher. But after that year I was hooked, mainly because the ministry for all its failings seemed a more important vehicle for allowing me to work with people. It was as simple as that; people first and God second.

I think what I am saying is that I began with my own needs and found them answered by the more traditional forms of religious experience. God, if He was going to use me at all, would perhaps do so through the agency of the parish church.

I had first been drawn to a chaplaincy — in school or college — and then summer hospital training revealed the possibility of service to the sick and dying. Crisis ministry, so to speak. Weekend "field-work" at Grace Church in South Boston opened up another option for me, that of a ministry to the poor. While my family managed to live better than some of those I grew up with, my home town and twelve years of public schooling were a mixed bag. I probably knew more poor people than I did rich ones. Besides, as my father's forty-year ministry in Winthrop revealed, less affluent people seemed to rely on the parson for many more things than those who could afford a lawyer, psychiatrist, adviser — all the things my father was to his flock and which I, in a much smaller way, was to the handful of the faithful in South Boston.

Then came a summer's job in a new mission in a booming construction town in eastern Oregon on the Columbia River. Later, when I was about to finish seminary and get ordained, I was invited to start my first full-time ministry there. I was tempted, and for the same reason that I was happy in South Boston: the people needed me. More than that, they actually wanted me as their minister. Had I gone to Hermiston, Oregon, in 1953, I'm sure I would have performed a useful ministry. These were people I only partly felt at home with, and yet who, like so many Westerners, were more open and warm than most of the New Englanders I had grown up with. The life in the West and subsequent years there would undoubtedly have made my career entirely different from what it now is.

Instead I started in a city parish in Providence, Rhode Island, one not unlike St. John's in Washington, a congregation of different kinds of people. There was a shortage of clergy and I had been offered jobs in New York City, Baltimore, and the Midwest; there were other equally attractive nibbles, but the curacy I accepted seemed to combine most of what I was looking for: a ministry to young people, to the sick, to the city poor, and to a variety of people in a wide variety of crises.

The downtown parish of Grace Church had its affluent members. Gradually Barbara and I found ourselves, a newly married couple, spending time with couples who had gone to Eastern colleges, who had some security in their backgrounds, and who were gradually making their way up in their several professions. I felt comfortable with many of these contemporaries — and with their parents. They seemed to respond to me, to my sermons when the rector let me preach, to my ideas, to the style of life which we tried to keep honest and free from the hypocrisy and self-aggrandizement I knew were always just below the surface of my life and the lives of other clergy I had known.

It wasn't that I lost interest in the underprivileged or ill-treated; it was simply that I discovered another aspect to the same ministry, still another group of people. The larger urban parish with its potential for power appealed to me no less than the smaller congregation where the minister's role was often more obvious. I discovered that I could help to effect change in the lives of different levels of society and not simply among the more limited group of people that I had previously known.

Some years later when I was called to become rector of Washington's St. John's I was glad for my experience in those former parishes which would help me to relate, however superficially, to the hundreds of people, mostly white, but by no means all rich or powerful, whose lives touch St. John's. As I say, I didn't start out to be a "society" rector, which to some extent Bedford's rector or the pastor of an important city church is. I genuinely want to serve people, and to the extent I understood then or do now the content of the Christian message I was drawn to a religious outlook in spite of those awful moments and experiences of my life which are in such contrast to the Gospel or when I have failed in a ministry to people who expect my help.

It would be foolish to think that what Bedford and perhaps Washington represent makes for a happier or more satisfying ministry. It doesn't. It was easier and more rewarding in many ways for me to be a big fish in a small pond than to serve in places where the ambiguities of the ministry are so subtle and where the personal temptations for me are so great. There is usually no "parson" in the city nor often among the sophisticated; the clergyman has to compete and to make his way on his own abilities, even though a healthy reliance on divine aid can be of enormous consequence and comfort. Life was a good deal easier and probably more pleasant at the start of my ministry than it is today at its midpoint. I was perhaps more effective then; certainly I was a less complicated person at thirty than I am as I approach fifty.

I enjoy the city, Washington in particular. I thrive on the challenge I receive from the pews on Sunday morning, from a wide variety of people who long for answers and who are unwilling to settle for words which do not reach them. Without always being aware of it, I am creatively confronted by attacks on my humanity by the people who come to St. John's or whom I meet professionally and socially. It is hard for me to get away with sloppy thinking or irrelevancy in my attitudes.

I know this only too well. Most of the time people who themselves are like me won't let me get away with easy answers or the undemanding action. They and I are part of a society where religion comes very hard and where what are called the Christian demands are ignored by so many of us because we are mightily afraid of their implications for our lives. People in a city like Washington are just as much in need of salvation as anyone else; yet the means of ministry to many of these people has to be different. I know this from personal experience because my own faith is constantly wavering and those supports I as an individual receive along the way are not always the ones we usually associate with the church. Certainly they are not always put in words or programs that my pastor father would understand or would himself have used in an otherwise deeply personal ministry in Winthrop a generation or more ago.

Because my parishioners expect me to challenge them in preaching and in counseling and to be aware of current events, ideas, and the nuances of twentieth-century life, I do a great deal of reading. This comes easily for me because literature, especially biography and novels, allows for some of the outlets which intimacy with actual people often makes so difficult. Strange. I am a minister because I want to help people better understand themselves, because I want to share with them my own humanity in their own deepest search for direction and meaning; and yet I often escape from this highly intense kind of relationship through my reading. I read at least a book a week — occasionally theology, seldom Biblical commentaries, more often some form of history — and I mark passages which can later be used in sermons and which my secretary copies on three-by-five cards.

Consequently, I have a large file of quotations which I use liberally in sermons — probably too much so. This may, however, be a way of my occasionally avoiding self-revelation, and who is to say quoting others is not a legitimate method of preaching? My cards are filed under such headings as "Human darkness," "Searching," "Pain," "Man's certainty," and "Prayer and the Spirit." It should not surprise anyone, least of all those who have known me as their preacher, that the cards for the first three categories outnumber the other two.

This is true of my reading in general, for I am more drawn to the lives of people who have suffered and sometimes have been defeated (Virginia Woolf, James Forrestal, Dag Hammarskjold, Samuel Drury of St. Paul's School come to mind) than to those physical and spiritual athletes who go through life without any apparent misgivings, mistakes, or serious defects. I try to read thoroughly the daily newspaper, weekly news magazines and the *New Yorker*, and while I am usually bored by strictly denominational magazines and articles about the church, I find controversial and ecumenical articles of genuine interest.

My friends sometimes accuse me of being an Anglophile, since much of my reading material comes from or concerns England. Strictly speaking, I am often critical of England, especially the Church of England, which I know from firsthand experience. At the same time I sense and thus value the bond which the history and traditions of Anglo-Saxon culture have given us. I feel comfortable with the English and to the extent that I understand it, our spiritual parent, the Church of England.

Through reading and summer travel abroad as well as exposure to some of those who are in positions of power and influence in this country I have tried to sharpen my mind to be an intelligent observer and occasionally a helpful interpreter of the times in which we live. I am neither a scholar nor a deep thinker; I am not especially original in what I have to say. I desperately need the stimulus of other people, personally or through their writings. I might have been more useful in a different kind of community than the one in which I now serve or among people whose need is more patently obvious; I might, although not necessarily, have become more humble and less complicated as a human being. But on the whole, I believe I have been of some help to people who like myself are caught in the haunted forest.

Chapter 9

———

THE TELEPHONE RANG almost as soon as I got home from church on Sunday noon. "Barbie, you answer it," I said from the dining room, where I was mixing martinis. "You answer and tell them I'm too drunk to talk or that I've gone to Bermuda or that I've dropped dead."

Over the years Barbie and I have come to an understanding about answering the telephone at home. For in a minister's house the telephone has a way of ringing at strange times and not always on important business. (Once a woman called in the middle of dinner and wanted to know the date of Christmas next year — so help me, she really did! — and people are always calling to find out the hour of church services. My family has become almost an automatic answering service: "Services 8, 9, and 11. Thank you. Goodbye.")

This time it was a serious call. I recognized the seriousness from Barbie's tone of voice. "Yes, Franny, he's here. Of course. Just a minute," Barbie said as she summoned me with a wave of her hand to the telephone in the hall. I put down the shaker of martinis without even having had a taste of what I hoped might be the "restorative brew" and came to the phone.

"It's Steve," Franny Rodgers said. "He's had a heart attack and is in the intensive care unit at the Hospital Center. Oh John," she began, and then started to cry. "Oh John, what's going to happen to him?"

Before I could say anything my mind began to race, and I'm afraid in circles rather than in a straight line. The Rodgerses are a couple we met through mutual friends when we first came to Washington. They are really our best friends. We see a lot of them. Steve's in the insurance business, and is exactly my age. Franny was pregnant when we first met, and after Timmy was born they asked me to be his godfather. I'm not much on acting as godfather because I've seen too many people like myself who've grown away from a particular family and never pay any attention to godchildren unless the wife goes out and buys a Christmas present. But I've gotten very fond of Timmy Rodgers, and he of me. He is only slightly younger than his two sisters, who always used to give him a hard time. Perhaps this was one reason why I was drawn to him in the first place. My older brother used to make my life miserable, as he still does sometimes. Yes, I have a certain amount of empathy for Timmy on that score alone.

Franny and Steve are my kind of people, with some of the same hangups that Barbie and I have. They're also people with a great deal of warmth and an enormous sense of humor. I like being with them almost more than with anyone else I know. Steve and I have nothing in common professionally; I don't know anything about insurance and I don't want to learn, and he's not interested in the nuances of theology, in what Tillich or Barth or whatever theologian I might be reading has to say about man and his world. (Franny and Barbie are more alike and were classmates at Smith.) In any case, there's a unique bond between the four of us which is something all of us cherish, even though none of us has ever really talked much *about* our relationship. It's close. We know it's close. We prefer to leave it at that.

But Steve with a coronary, in the intensive care unit, sick, maybe going to die . . . It was more than I could take in all at once. Steve has always been the stronger of us, the outdoors type, in perfect physical condition, full of energy and drive. And now my best friend in Washington was about to die.

Franny's sobs brought me back to reality. Steve wasn't necessarily going to die, I knew. I was jumping too fast. Lots of men in their late forties have heart attacks and survive. In fact, I remember a doctor saying facetiously that every male ought to have some heart disease before he's fifty to make him slow up and face reality. It's just that Steve and I are the same age, that I care for him and Franny, and that the unknown over the telephone made me lose my bearings for a few seconds.

It's hard to be someone's friend and his minister as well. That's why a minister's family ought to have someone else as their pastor, although I doubt if many do. I suspect most clergymen's families go doggedly to church every Sunday, see their husband or father up front, and get terribly confused about his role as holy man and the man they know at home who's a whiz as a lover, or a martinet, or an ambitious son-of-a-bitch, or a total failure as a family man. I've been in this business long enough to know that wives can be terribly confused about their roles and that children of clergymen often have to rebel against their fathers in order to figure out their own religious commitments (as well as for all the other reasons kids rebel). Sometimes they go the opposite extreme from the old man and become thoroughly indifferent to religion and refuse to go to church, as I did during the war and for several years afterward. Sometimes a wife will go into psychotherapy in order to help her deal with her feelings about the various roles she must share with her minister-husband.

But whatever the response on the part of the family, I know from experience that I can't be a really effective counselor to people I know too well, either to my family or my friends. Most of my parishioners I have met on a professional level first, and some of them have become friends. It's rarely been the other way around; very few of the people I've known well socially later become part of my professional life. It's just too risky for both sides. They go elsewhere to church.

The Rodgerses are an exception to this even though Steve often finds golf on Sunday more inspirational than my sermons. He comes to church for important occasions or when I suggest it's high time he showed his face on Sunday morning. But my main contacts with him are at lunch during the week, on the squash court, and of course when the four of us get together for drinks or dinner. It had somehow never really occurred to me that someday I might have to try to help Steve or Franny in a clerical sense.

"I'll be at the hospital as soon as I can get there," I said to Franny, when I discovered that she was calling from the phone at the nurses' station on the floor. "Hold on. Nothing's going to happen to Steve."

Why not? Because the Reverend John Carsten Harper, D.D., with his bag of magical tricks, is on the way? Because God never takes off a healthy father of three wonderful children and a loving husband? Because I have all the answers and can do something to relieve the situation? What do I know about what's going to happen to Steve? Will my prayers reverse the course of heart disease or forestall another heart attack? Can I keep the other shoe from dropping?

Barbie wanted to come with me to the hospital, but I wouldn't let her. She wanted to be with Franny, but something in me wanted to take over, to do my job alone. It was unfair to Barbie — but I felt helpless about Steve and the only thing I could hope to do was to give some support to Franny. That would ease some of the guilt a minister feels when people turn to him in crises and he knows there's nothing to be done but pray. Maybe if I reached through to Franny I'd be reaching through to Steve too. If only I were a medical doctor. Well, I could stand by Franny for a while. That was something.

It wasn't until I was halfway to the hospital that I remembered the martinis. I was glad I hadn't had a drink, because I don't like to be around people who're not drinking when I've had one. The martinis wouldn't have made me any sharper, either, or given me any more courage to face one of my best friends.

I knew of a doctor once who was called out from dinner to see a sick child of some friends of mine, and they told me later that he said to them when they called him, "I'll come if you want me, but I think you ought to know that I've had a cocktail. If that makes a difference to you, I'll try to find someone else to come." That was over twenty years ago, and I've never forgotten that remark. The doctor was not only a very sensible man but an honest one. I admit a doctor has specific skills he brings to a patient that alcohol may impede; where the minister has words, just words. But if that's all the minister has to offer, he'd better be damn sure the words are his own clear words and not muddled or misdirected by too much booze.

Franny was leaning against the wall outside the swinging glass doors of the intensive care unit when I arrived at the hospital. She looked terribly small and frightened.

"The doctor's in there now," she said as I took her in my arms and kissed her. "Oh, John," she said, and like our conversation on the telephone a few minutes before, her words ended in sobs.

Franny and I have been close to each other over the last nine years, and whatever fantasies I've had about being in love with another woman have centered around her. Ministers, like everyone else, do have these fantasies, and sometimes they act them out. In my case, I hadn't, although it isn't because I haven't thought about it. But I know Franny cares a lot about me. She once told me so when I stopped by the Rodgerses' house late in the afternoon, when I knew Steve wouldn't be there or the children either. Franny is like a sister to me. Or is that all? Sometimes I don't dare trust my feelings about her.

"Steve's going to be all right," I said, almost as a refrain to Franny's own repetitious cry for help. What else was there to say to her? But what did I know anyway about the heart or illness or people — or anything for that matter?

A couple of years ago I went through a similar crisis, only that time it was with someone I didn't think I cared much about one way or the other — but someone who cared a great deal about me. She was a lonely single woman at St. John's by the name of Agnes Hammond and she lived on Sixteenth Street in a room on the third floor of another parishioner's home. She had a menial job in some government office, and I remember the first day she turned up at St. John's. We get a lot of these lonely people who gravitate to the city church in hopes of making friends and of having someone to talk to, and that's precisely why Agnes came. Only she was too shy to talk. She simply came because she wanted to be in the presence of other people. She felt she had nothing to give them; their life around her at the coffee hour and in the church itself was what mattered. She liked to watch them and listen to them talk.

I got to know her, and in her shy, inarticulate way she told me she'd never been baptized and would like to be. And so we had a private service, with my secretary present, and Agnes was officially "received into the household of God." Only it wasn't a very welcoming household, because most people at St. John's didn't pay any attention to her and I usually had other things on my mind on Sunday mornings.

Sensing she needed something to do, I asked her if she'd mind answering the telephone in the parish office during the Sunday morning coffee hour.

There was enough commotion around the office and enough people were drifting in and out after the service to give her some interest, and the occasional calls that did come through to the church gave her an incentive to speak to someone, usually to me.

It was while minding the telephone on Sunday that Agnes had a heart attack. We sat her down in a chair as we waited for the ambulance and while Agnes in a plaintive way kept sobbing, "God, please don't let me die." I took her in my arms like a child, while people stood around wanting to help but not knowing what to do. I kept saying to her, "It's all right, Agnes; it's all right."

This frightened, lonely woman had only me to love her. There were just two of us together: an unattractive woman who had no one else to care about her, and me. The people around us didn't count; they didn't matter to Agnes or to me at that moment. When we got to the hospital and she was taken to the emergency room I went with her, and I was holding her hand when she died on the examining table, still saying to her, "It's all right, Agnes; it's all right."

She trusted me to stay with her, and I did. Only I hadn't really cared for Agnes until it was almost too late. I pray she knew in those final minutes that someone did care. I pray my caring made up for some of the long years of her terrible loneliness.

Would it be like that now with Steve? Would I tell him that I loved him before it was too late, and would we ever meet in the way I had finally met with Agnes by one of us saying to the other, "It'll be all right," and the other knowing that no matter what would happen the words were true?

I waited with Franny to see the doctor who told us that Steve was doing OK, that the next couple of days would be critical ones. Dr. Kingman knows me well enough to realize that I could stick my head in the door, say hello, and get out of the way without unduly disturbing a patient. He also realized that Steve would like to know I was around.

"Go on in," he said, "but just for a minute." Together Franny and I entered the room where Steve was lying. He managed a thin smile and made some sly comment to the effect that this was God's way of punishing him for not being in church this morning and for playing golf instead at Chevy Chase. I started to touch him, to put my hand on his arm or on his head, anywhere so long as I could assure him — and myself — that we could communicate with each other. I wanted to show him by some physical gesture, like taking Agnes into my arms, that I loved him. But it wasn't the time to do that. He was too sick.

"Steve, we're with you, old friend . . . we're praying for you."

When I said that I suddenly realized that in the half hour or so that I'd known of Steve's illness I'd not prayed for him at all. Perhaps Franny had; perhaps his children at home were praying; maybe Barbie was. But I hadn't. I'd thought a lot about him, about what might happen. But I'd not said any kind of a conscious prayer.

"Steve, I'm going to ask God to see you through this," I said lamely and in my heart guiltily. Taking his hand and Franny's I mumbled in some embarrassment: "O God, make Steve well again; help him to trust in your mercy; help him to know that underneath are the Everlasting Arms. Amen."

The last part about the Everlasting Arms is corny maybe, and it occurred to me as I said the words it would sound trite, churchy, to Steve. Yet the Everlasting Arms (mine and God's) were just what I wanted to believe in at that moment. They were what I was counting on to pull Steve through his heart attack. They were the means of showing him that we care about him, and although Steve may not have realized it, it was the most honest prayer I'd prayed all day.

Chapter 10

M OST MINISTERS now have some clinical pastoral training as part of their seminary education. The trouble is that we often have a lot — but seldom enough. As a result, we think we know more than we actually do about medical and psychiatric disorders, and we can make some very serious mistakes in dealing with people. Lacking a sufficiently thorough education, lacking experience, we can easily be taken in, especially by people who are out to con us.

I spent two summers in clinical training, one at the Worcester State Mental Hospital and the other at the Massachusetts General Hospital in Boston.

Both experiences were among the best I had in seminary and each in its own way convinced me that I wanted to work with people.

A lot of what most clergy do is gut reaction and good common sense. My father, who was completely untrained in the techniques of pastoral counseling, nevertheless had a great deal of horse sense which stood him in good stead and allowed him to remain rector of the same parish for forty years, which says a lot about him and about the patience of his parishioners. Once, just before Christmas, a distraught woman came to him and said she planned to kill herself. Pausing for a moment to light his pipe, my father replied, "That's perfectly all right; I don't blame you at all after what you've been through. But you'll have to wait until after Christmas, because I don't have time before that to conduct your funeral."

So far as I know she's still living. At least she was a few years ago when I heard she had gone to my father's successor with the same threat and was into deep, twice-a-week counseling with that man. Maybe it would have been better for her if my father had known more about the inner workings of hysterical women. Maybe it's just as well he didn't. In either case, the woman has had a delightful time in the new minister's study over the past five years, and the present rector feels he's being useful.

The seminarian's encounter with mental illness not only helps him to recognize symptoms in his parishioners (pity the poor people in the fledgling parson's parish where everyone becomes a "case"), but it also helps him to understand something about himself, to be more accepting of deviations from what is generally considered the norm, and to learn some patience with the moods and behavior of other human beings. The Worcester State Hospital was a great experience for me, as it has been for countless other seminarians since the program was founded many years ago. (It was the first of such programs in the country.) The hospital administrator gathered us together one evening, while thunder and lightning ominously bombarded the tower room where we were meeting. "Don't be naïve," were his opening words to us. "These patients will try to make you believe there's nothing wrong with them, and sometimes that will appear to be the case. They'll try to get you to intercede with us to let them go home. But don't be naïve. Don't be naïve."

I thought then that he was trying to justify his administration of that large hospital and was trying to make it clear that we were to be on the side of the establishment and not of the patients. What he said turned out to be good advice, though. I've since realized that his words were more profound than he may have known. Clergy, indeed, are often terribly naïve about the people we see. We're supposed, some think, to see good in everybody. If it is also true that some clergy are terribly cynical, this may be because over the years they've been had by any number of plausible-sounding and -appearing people who try to take them in.

Suspicious though I am of people who come in off the street to ask for help at St. John's, I've had my share of con artists. A young man came in to see me one day asking for pastoral help. He was, he said, a promiscuous homosexual, the son of a clergyman. He was lonely in Washington and wanted someone to talk to about his troubles. He wanted to be straight, he told me, and he hoped I could help him. We talked for over an hour and as he was leaving, with an appointment to return again next week, he turned and said, "I wonder if you could loan me some money." I smelled a rat, but I figured, what the hell, he'd seemed to be honest with me and I might as well help him out with money from my discretionary fund. The upshot: I never saw him again. There wasn't any such man in the ministry as he claimed for his father, and I was out twenty-five bucks.

Or the time a man came in for confession (a rarity in my parish) and I heard him, sitting solemnly in front of him in one of the pews of the darkened church while he poured out a story of woe which would make any priest blush. When it was over, he politely said, "Father, do you have a discretionary fund?" Naïvely I replied, "But there's no charge; I'm glad to be of some help to you." I didn't add "my son," but at thirty-two I might have.

"Father, I don't want to give something to it," the man said, "I want to borrow some money." Later, after I'd lent him ten dollars, I discovered from two other ministers in town that he'd hit them for money too after a wonderfully exciting confession the likes of which we Protestant ministers don't usually get.

"Don't be naïve," said the administrator at Worcester, and the advice still holds after all these years.

When I came to Washington I was warned by another clergyman about a particular couple who, he said, were the two biggest con artists in the city and who had recently transferred to my parish. Sure enough, they were in my office before the week was out and in the course of six months I expended three hundred dollars and untold hours in their behalf. Finally, I kicked them out of the office one day when I couldn't take it any longer. I've not seen them since.

What's happened to them, I wonder? Some other pastor in Washington is no doubt spending his time and money on them until his naïveté or patience runs out. That's the bind the clergyman is in, of course. He's in business to help — in appropriate ways. But people don't always understand that occasionally the best medicine for someone is to give him a good kick and tell him to get out. Or tell the neurotic suicidal woman that you haven't time to conduct her funeral. But that's treading on thin ice. I don't recommend it. Sometimes people who are genuinely looking for help go away empty when the clergyman's defenses are up or he hasn't the time to listen or he guesses wrong.

I am most uneasy in those situations when my clinical training seems to provide me with answers and when later I turn out to be wrong. I've never been one for permissive counseling; that's the psychiatrist's role, a necessary one in long-term therapy. The kind of counseling I do tends to be short-range, and when a problem seems beyond my scope I turn to more professional help. I've seen a lot of good results and I've worked with some very effective analysts and psychiatric counselors in Washington. But there are occasions when I myself produce what seem to me to be answers, and often either the advice I give is wrong or the occasion ill-timed.

Several years ago I'd been seeing off and on a middle-aged woman who was married to an older, alcoholic husband. Their marriage was terrible from every point of view. My knowledge of them both had become quite extensive, and the more I saw of them individually and together the more I was convinced that she should pull up stakes and leave him, as she'd threatened on a number of occasions to do. She was a whiner, though. Every time I tried to suggest a practical solution to what was probably an insoluble relationship, she'd counter with another proposal or say that Millard needed her. Which was probably true.

She went into the hospital for a gallbladder operation one day and I stopped by to see her the night before her operation. I had plenty of time and so I sat with her in the hospital room and listened to what had long since become a familiarly dreary recital of troubles between her and Millard. After an hour of the same stuff, I finally exploded and told her that if she didn't leave her husband there was no hope for either of them, that I was sick and tired of hearing her complaints, that the best thing she could do was to shut up and act for once like a mature person. I left the room in anger and went home.

The next morning I had a call from the woman's psychiatrist, also a woman, who tore me to shreds on the telephone. Did I realize I'd acted in the most unprofessional way possible, upsetting a patient the night before an operation, telling her under those tense circumstances things which I had no right to say?

If it's possible to hang one's head while talking on the telephone, I did. I was deeply ashamed of myself, even though I still believed that what I had said was true. Had I scarred the poor woman for the rest of her life? Had I lost my professional grip?

I guess both those things happened. But when the woman recovered from her operation she left town and moved to another part of the country, where her two children for the first time in their lives have a decent home. The last time I heard about her, she had a good job and was beginning to recoup some of the money that Millard had been siphoning off for the past ten years. Maybe I helped her after all.

And Millard? I don't know about him, and one part of me hopes he's at the bottom of the Potomac River for the way he's behaved. I never see him around Washington, although I occasionally look for him in some of the places I used to find him. He doesn't come to church anymore; he doesn't wake me up in the middle of the night when he's drunk; he doesn't interfere with my life the way he used to. But then he does still interfere because I can't forget that in one sense I failed them both.

One of the great values in the seminarian's hospital training is to learn some of his own inner weaknesses and to make some decisions about them. The anger that so many of us have within us can be deadly and destructive, and can spill over onto the people with whom we have to deal. This is one reason why so many seminarians and clergy have had some personal experience with psychoanalysis or some other form of psychotherapy. If treatment helps the minister learn more about how to help others it's worth the money and effort. If it helps him to learn more about himself, then therapy's a must, and it's the wise minister who accepts this as a part of his personal as well as his professional life. It need not always be a psychiatrist, of course. But it must be a trained professional who understands and has treated other human beings effectively.

A minister by his work is forced not only to deal with troubled people but with himself. He has to be in touch with his own feelings, and often this is not possible unless he is willing to uncover a lot that over the years has been hidden from sight. Then he can begin to be a loving, less threatened help to the Millards of this world who in one way or another cross his path.

When I stood in the hospital corridor with Franny and when I went into Steve's hospital room for that brief visit on Sunday noon, I was doing something which every minister does thousands of times. The clergyman has had a lot of experience in hospital calling and knows some techniques, and he is ready for an encounter of some depth with the patient. Sometimes he does what comes naturally, which is to say he says hello and lets the chips fall where they may. He learns, although he may not practice it, when to be quiet and listen, and he becomes familiar with hospital routine, recognizing appropriate and inappropriate times in which to visit a sick person.

I spent a fascinating summer term at the Massachusetts General Hospital, where as part of our training we were expected to observe one operation and one autopsy each day. This program had essentially two objectives: it made us more or less accustomed to the ugliness of sickness and death (my first autopsy was of a beautiful eighteen-year-old girl who had died of a mysterious fever, and the doctors were trying, in my frightened presence, to find the cause) and, secondly, it helped us learn something about such familiar operations as hysterectomies and appendectomies — or even more dramatic operations like brain or heart surgery. When a parishioner tells me she's to have a mastectomy I at least know what she's talking about, and I know from watching several of them something about the surgical procedure. I know, too, what goes on in an operating room and inside hospitals generally.

At the Mass. General they started us out for two weeks as orderlies on the wards. I learned to empty bedpans, make beds, and take people to the operating room. One old man said to me one day as I was giving him his morning enema: "Sonny, you give the best goddamn enemas in this hospital." High praise indeed.

Of course it's possible to learn too much as a layman and think one knows it all, to become neurotically fascinated by illness, so that one becomes an amateur diagnostician. You've heard the story of the automobile accident and of the woman who came along and began to give first aid to the victim. After she'd worked over him for a few minutes, a doctor drove up and was impressed by her acumen as she gave him the facts: "Blood pressure is 120 over 80; pulse is 90; bleeding is under control."

"Are you a nurse?" the doctor asked the good samaritan.

"No," was the reply, "I'm a hypochondriac."

So are many clergy who nevertheless minister effectively to sick people. We are drawn to illness for many reasons, not the least of which is that we have sympathy — and empathy — for those who are ill. In a perfectly acceptable way their pain becomes our own, and the more we learn about theirs the more we learn about our own. Or to reverse it, if we have some understanding of our own physical strengths and limitations we may be better able to share this knowledge with others in their need.

Once at the Massachusetts Eye and Ear Infirmary,

which is part of the larger Mass. General, we seminarians were watching an eye operation. Gowned like the young doctors who were performing the operation, we stood around the table. Occasionally the head surgeon would look over at one of my fellow seminarians, apparently to show him what he was doing, and my classmate would nod his head to indicate he understood. When the operation was almost over, a nurse opened the door to the operating room and called in: "Don't start the operation. Dr. Lowry will be late."

The young surgeon put down his instrument in horrified disbelief and turned to my classmate: "But aren't *you* Dr. Lowry?" he gasped.

He'd taken the approving nods as signals from the great Lowry when all the time he'd been operating on his own.

I'm glad to say the operation was a success and the patient made an uneventful recovery. My seminarian friend, instead of going into eye surgery, is now rector of a parish in California and visits in the hospital — I'm told without a white gown. The Massachusetts Eye and Ear Infirmary continues to be a great hospital where young doctors are well trained, although not by seminarians as a usual thing.

Steve Rodgers didn't ask me how sick he was when I went in to see him. People rarely do. They know. People don't usually ask whether they're going to die, although patients do sometimes ask this of doctors or ministers or members of their families. The critically ill person has a right to ask questions or not as he sees fit, and no one should enter his life without being asked to. I've seen extraordinary people die without ever once asking whether they have cancer or whether the time for them is short.

There was Susie Henry whom I saw each day for a month in her home as she grew weaker and weaker. We didn't fool each other, but neither did we discuss the inevitability of her death. I wish now we had, for my sake and for hers. We spent a lot of time talking about her three married children, who are all good friends of mine, about St. John's, and some of the things I was doing. We talked about my family, in which she always had a lively interest. Occasionally we prayed, although not to make her well but to give her courage to bear her sufferings.

That was as near as we ever got to mentioning the cancer, which until the last two weeks, even her closest friends who visited her never discussed among themselves. They knew she was sick but they didn't know she was dying.

I was enormously fond of Susie. When she finally did die, I went over to the house and knelt by the bed of that wasted, almost unrecognizable figure, and my own mother's death from cancer and all the other deaths of people I've cared about came flooding over me. Susie wasn't just another person. She had allowed me into her life because I was first her minister and then, after I had proved myself, her friend. Steve too had let me into his life, only in his case I was there only as his friend, to give him what sense of peace I could just by my being there, but not as a minister offering whatever comfort our religion and our Church might have to give.

I'm often puzzled by what the Church really does have to offer sick people like Susie Henry and Steve Rodgers. Not just thoughts of heaven certainly. In the case of Susie, I took her the Holy Communion several times and this gave her great comfort, as it would me. She was a good Christian and understood what the Church offered in the tangible gift of the Sacraments.

But Steve wasn't that kind of person; I don't know what went on in his mind last Easter when he came to Holy Communion and knelt at the altar rail. Probably he was both reverent and irreverent; awed a little and hoping he'd feel better, maybe even be a better person for the experience of receiving the Holy Communion, but also slightly mocking of the taste of the unleavened bread and wondering whether the priest at the altar ever got tight when he drank the remaining wine.

Susie wouldn't have had these thoughts; at least I don't think she would. But Steve would. If he lives, he may want to talk about himself, his family, and his future — and none of the religious props that I'm used to will be much help. He'll be looking for some direct, hard answers. I'd like to have some of the right ones for him.

Chapter 11

I WONDER what it's like to die. My father slipped away into the comforting arms of senility and went quietly into the night, not raging "against the dying of the light." Others do everything they can to stay alive; they go to an array of doctors, submit to operations, take the drugs and the radiation therapy in an attempt to keep life going a little longer, sometimes long after their weakened bodies have any right to exist at all. Others die suddenly and without warning — often in the prime of life. That kind of death is the hardest of all for a minister to cope with.

Billy Howard's parents called me at the Cape during my vacation last summer to tell me of their tragedy. Billy, at summer camp in New Hampshire, had gone mountain climbing in Pinkham Notch in the White Mountains and had fallen to his death from a ledge overlooking Tuckerman's Ravine.

I was stunned when Matt Howard told me over the phone of his son's death. Billy, my own son Jeff's age, was one of the most promising and attractive boys I knew. He was as devoted to his parents and three brothers and two sisters as anyone could be. The Howard family was an unusually close one.

"Would you be able to come up to our place in Conway and conduct a memorial service for Billy?" Matt Howard asked hesitantly. "It'll just be the family and a few of his friends. Maybe you'd like to bring Jeff with you. I know this is your vacation, John, so if it's not convenient, just say so. But I wanted you to know. I . . ."

"Of course, I'll be there, Matt." I said. "And Jeff too." I knew full well what Billy's death was going to mean to my son.

I put down the receiver and began to think what I was going to say to Jeff when he returned from tennis. Billy's been killed in an accident, Jeff; your friend Billy is dead; you won't see him again; Billy fell to his death without warning, and Billy's family there in Conway, New Hampshire, are calling other family members and friends to tell them what's happened. Jeff, I can't really tell you what's happened, because even I, a guy who's supposed to be good at understanding these things, don't know. I don't know why this happened to Billy. Or why a wonderful family of a father, mother, and now five children should be hurting today in the way they hurt. I don't know what it's like to die any more than I know why something like this happens to people you and I know. I only know that Billy's dead and that you and I have been asked to help him. Well, not him maybe, but by helping his family we're doing something for Billy too. Let's go, Jeff, but remember, stop asking yourself why it happened. Stop asking me what it's like to die or what it's like for Billy now.

We drove up to Conway, to a farm which I'd known as a boy. (My parents spent part of their summers at a place nearby.) It seemed natural to leave the state road and turn onto the winding dirt road which led past the Littlefield farm and up Potters' hill and then, after a sweeping view of the Presidential Range, to turn into the woods again before the last quarter of a mile to the Howards' summer place.

Jeff and I didn't say very much to each other, and now that we were almost there talk seemed irrelevant. Both of us were thinking now about the Howards and what meeting them was going to be like, and what to say to them about Billy.

Matt came out to greet us, doing his best to smile. We met the rest of the family, friends we had known so well, and yet who, even in that familiar setting, seemed so alien. It was unnatural to be there in my city clothes, for one thing; I realized I'd never worn a necktie in my whole life around Conway, never had on hard-soled shoes as I did this warm August morning. That was one reason why it seemed strange to be there, even among people I knew and loved.

But then I realized another, more obvious reason for my uneasiness. Someone was missing. Billy. I'd spent a lot of time with the Howards, and without realizing it we'd seen them mostly as an entire family, and that meant Billy too. The rest were there on the screened porch this morning for the simple memorial service, but Billy wasn't around. It wasn't just his body that was missing, a crushed body which earlier had been cremated and which would later that fall be buried in the family plot in Washington. I wasn't thinking of the dead Billy at all but of the live, vibrant boy I'd known for the last decade, Jeff's friend and mine. The family circle had a hole in it, and nothing I could do or say would make up for the loss.

"We're here this morning," I began, "to remember Billy. . . ." What a silly way to start a memorial service, I thought to myself; of course that's why we're here; how can we ever forget him, the boy who was senior prefect last year at Potomac School, who alternated with Jeff as captain of the baseball team, who one time drove my car down Bancroft Place, a one-way street, in the wrong direction and without my permission. Of course we're here to remember a sandy-haired kid who brought such fun into our lives. But that's right; we do this because we want to be honest about Billy. We're here to remember him today and always, to promise each other that we won't forget him.

"We're here," I continued, "for another, even better reason, and that's to say thank you in our own way for what Billy means to us, each of us, to you his family and to us his friends. Each of us has some reason to be grateful that we knew Billy, and now we've gathered here in this place which he loved so much to say that from our own hearts. Only I'll have to do most of the talking for you; that's why I'm here, one of the reasons anyway, to try to put into words what we all mean when we say that we thank God for a life of someone close to us and that we're willing now to give him back to God who gave him to us in the first place."

"I am the resurrection and the life, saith the Lord; he that believeth in me shall never die. . . ."

"For I am persuaded that neither death nor life . . . can separate us. . . ."

"For love is immortal, and death is only a horizon, and a horizon is nothing save the limit of our sight."

We ended the service for Billy in silence on the big porch of the summer house overlooking the White Mountains ("I will lift up mine eyes unto the hills"), which had brought such peace to so many in this place and yet which also were the cause now of the tragedy that brought us together. There wasn't any more to say after the final prayers had been spoken and we had joined hands, the dozen or so of us who were present, and stood in a circle. We were linked then in a curious way, and for the first time that day I sensed that Billy was present after all; the circle was no longer an imperfect one. Those who joined their hands together didn't need to say anything more. We were together there, human beings touching one another and touched by an absent friend who shared that moment with us.

One of the most pleasant duties a minister has is to officiate at the marriage of older men and women, widows and widowers, who in their later years have found one another and want to commit themselves to each other for the remaining years they may have. Rachel and Ernest were just such a couple. Each had been married before and each had lost a spouse from cancer. They were in their sixties, and their children were simply delighted at the prospect of this second marriage. Years before during their first marriages they had been good friends and had shared much together. It seemed right now to their families and friends for Rachel and Ernest to be married, and so we had a wedding with champagne and toasts and grandchildren taking part in the service. If there was ever a family wedding, this was it.

Rachel and Ernest departed on a long trip around the world which would be culminated a year later by a six months' stay at Rachel's house outside Paris. During the time they were away I heard from them, and from Rachel's scribbled postcards and Ernest's letters I sensed that this was truly a happy marriage, and I was grateful that I'd had even a symbolic part in helping to make it so.

I was spending that summer at the American Cathedral in Paris, and Barbie and I went out several times to see what I called "my happy bride and groom." Then one morning Rachel telephoned to say that Ernest had had a massive heart attack during the night and was dead. Rachel needed to make arrangements for the funeral, and she wondered if it could be held at the American Cathedral, since they had so many friends in Paris. Of course, I said. Rachel and I met early on the morning of the funeral in the church. While Ernest's body lay there before the altar, the two of us sat quietly in the front pew and talked about how happy they'd been together and what the past sixteen months had meant to them.

"But they're not over," Rachel firmly said, when I made some mention of her loss. "It's not going to end now."

And so the funeral service came to be a great outpouring of thanksgiving for two people, not just for one, and for the love which found them and which bound them together even for so short a time. It was a great act of thanksgiving and also of praise, and I marveled at Rachel's faith and also at her very real sense of joy for what had been. What was now would have to be sorted out, the grief and sense of loss dealt with at another time. At the moment, in the presence of the family and some friends who had loved them both, she wanted to give the same kind of thanks to God as they together had given at the wedding. And she did.

Just before the service began Rachel made a strange request. "You were a part of our wedding, John, and you're now a part of Ernest's funeral. You stood with us at the wedding. Won't you stand with me at the door of the Cathedral at the end of the service so that together in Ernest's name we can greet our friends?"

At the conclusion of the funeral, therefore, I went down to the front pew, and gave my arm to Rachel, and together she and I walked slowly down the aisle of the Cathedral to the front door, where we greeted members of the congregation. I stood there beside her in my vestments.

I wasn't sure I was going to make it, but Rachel had no doubt for herself at all. With her head held high and with the honest graciousness that is a part of her life, she told each person who came up to us how grateful she was for their coming, and then to each, and with different words, she spoke of her love for Ernest and of his love for her. Death, where is thy sting?

It was this way last year when a young mother died after a long illness, and I walked to the grave with her husband and four children, the youngest barely ten years old. We all had cried at the pain of Laurie's death and at what the removal of a strong mother would mean to this family which so depended on her. No death seemed more senseless, and the family that was left behind to pick up the threads of their lives again seemed utterly lost. They were lost that day as we numbly turned away from the grave and went back to our cars. Little Sis dropped her father's hand and turning back toward the grave for just a second, said in strong tones, "Goodbye, Mommie; thank you for all you did for us." That was better than any blessing I might have said. It was a blessing of thanksgiving from one who knew what she had received.

Life goes on, of course, for the family who has lost a child or a parent, for one who has lost a lover or a friend. Funerals aren't the only special services a minister conducts; or weddings like the one I will conduct for Linda and Michael, or baptisms, either. There are also the special events that ministers get themselves into, some of them very "special" indeed.

Several years ago we returned from Europe on the *United States*. I prefer to travel as "Mr." rather than as "Reverend," which may say something negative about my commitment to the Gospel. Or it just may be common sense to be off duty for a little while.

I say facetiously that my reason for not flaunting my collar while traveling is if the boat sinks I can be first off and not have to wait patiently as a Christian for the women and children to go first. The real reason is that I sometimes enjoy anonymity, and I was especially looking forward to five days of complete relaxation at sea.

However, the first day out the purser, somehow discovering that I was a clergyman, asked me if I'd conduct the Sunday service in the first-class movie theater.

"Don't you have some big-shot cleric on board?" I asked him; "some bishop or cardinal?"

"Frankly, no," was the honest reply. "You're the only clergyman on the ship."

"Well, how about the captain? Isn't that the kind of thing he's supposed to do?"

The purser hesitated, and it occurred to me by his silence that the captain's talents did not include the conduct of divine service.

"It will be a great feather in your cap," was his final word. I didn't feel I needed that kind of feather, but I agreed to conduct the service.

It was obvious later that day that the captain, although not particularly liking to conduct church services, knew that a storm was coming and that he'd probably be needed on the bridge. Anyway, that's what happened, and from Thursday to Saturday most of the passengers, including the Sunday parson, were confined to their staterooms. By Sunday the sea had somewhat abated, and I struggled to the movie theater to sing "Nearer, My God, To Thee," or whatever the hymn was, and to preach the sermon standing at a lectern on the stage in front of a large curtain.

The ship's orchestra was seated behind the curtain, presumably out of view. What neither they nor I realized, but what was quite obvious to the sparse congregation, was that the curtain would sway with the motion of the ship and that while I was fervently praying or telling my listeners about the perils of life's seas, the orchestra was having a fine old time drinking beer, making obscene gestures at one another and perhaps at me. I was glad when the service ended if for no other reason than I was beginning to feel seasick again. I sensed too that my listeners had had other distractions. Barbie confirmed this as we struggled back to the stateroom.

"You were great," she loyally said, "but not nearly as much fun as the orchestra. You should have seen them."

I'm glad I didn't; I'm not sure I would have continued. I don't like other people spoiling my act, especially when I have a feather in my cap.

On the ship that time was an old lady I'd come to know well as one of my parishioners in Bedford. She had long been a widow and lived quietly in a small house in the country, traveling every summer to England to visit her young nieces and nephews. She had no family in the United States, and except for two very proper lady friends in Bedford she was quite alone. She attended the service that morning on the ship and she often went to church at St. Matthew's.

Shortly after Christmas she became ill, and in the early spring she died. Her two Bedford friends came to see me about her funeral. Mrs. Smithfield was, I knew, devout and would want the Burial Office from the Prayer Book just the way it was written, without any deletions or additions, but I did suggest that perhaps I might read the shorter Scripture Lesson from the Epistle to the Romans since, as I told her friends, the one from Corinthians is "rather long and confusing."

Miss Bryce drew herself up in her chair and said to me: "Young man, I want you to know that the word of God is never too long *or* confusing!"

So we had Corinthians, Romans, and everything else Thomas Cranmer or whoever it was put in the Book of Common Prayer. It wasn't confusing at all, just as Miss Bryce said, except that I thought, when we came to the end of the passage in which St. Paul cautions us to be "steadfast, unmoveable," of the old parish Warden who'd served for fifty-three years and whose memorial tablet bore those words, and I thought of Miss Bryce herself, who wasn't going to be moved by any young minister with new ideas about shortening or trying to make more intelligible the Word of God.

We scattered Mrs. Smithfield's ashes in the outdoor Chapel-in-the-Woods, while Miss Bryce and her friend carefully watched to see that all was done correctly. My dog Dusty followed along behind, with other thoughts on her mind. All I could think of as I distributed Mrs. Smithfield's remains was Millet's famous painting of the sower and of an appropriate caption for that work of art and for me: "Easy come, easy go."

Which is perhaps not a bad way of describing the

entrance and exit of Christian souls from this world. Miss Bryce wouldn't have liked that. It's too short a description of life's pilgrimage. But I think Mrs. Smithfield would understand. So, I believe, would God.

Chapter 12

BY THE TIME I got home from visiting Steve at the hospital I'd forgotten about lunch, martinis, and Linda Bentley and Michael Laskey. Steve and death were too much on my mind. I really didn't think he was going to die, but I was frightened. In spite of what that doctor said, people shouldn't have heart attacks at forty-eight.

It was four o'clock and I needed some time to be alone. Barbie's questions about Steve I would deal with summarily, much to her rightful annoyance.

"Look, Barbie," I finally said to her after I'd gone through the brief facts for the second time, "that's all anybody knows at this point. We've got to keep our fingers crossed and hope he'll be all right." With that I went upstairs to the study off our bedroom, shut the door and turned on the radio to hear the last of a concert by the Boston Symphony.

I could see in my mind's eye the two drunks I'd passed earlier in the day on my way to church, sick men like Steve who either didn't want help or weren't asking for it. Like Steve they couldn't be reached. The doctor wasn't going to make Steve instantly well, was he? No social worker, minister, or AA member was going to take away the sickness of those two characters I passed on the street this morning, either. In a sense, both they and Steve were going to have to make it on their own. That is what's so hard.

I can't reach them no matter how many good intentions or pastoral tricks or prayers I might have in my minister's bag. The drunks, like any emotionally disturbed person, have got to want to get help and have got to take the first step and perhaps all the steps on their own. No one can make them stop drinking, or stop in a way that means anything to them. And no one can cure Steve, although there are a number of specific things that professional people can do.

As a clergyman, one of the aids I rely on is prayer. I'm not always sure of prayer, at least not the kind of prayer I was taught in seminary. When I don't pray I feel guilty. I don't do well praying on my own, which may be why I felt empty and drained right then, sitting in my study looking out on the tennis court across the street at four players who were not thinking about any of this. I can't shift gears very easily, from the hospital to home, from trying to pray with a sick friend and his wife to being by myself.

Nevertheless, even in my own study, I'm surrounded by so many evidences of other people and their caring for me. The pictures on the wall; the faces of six of my former assistants who gave me a party and their pictures four years ago on the fifteenth anniversary of my ordination, or the church in Bedford, New York, where I last served and which was such a warm, loving community of people. I try to make myself believe that I got through to those people in Bedford more effectively because my faith was less complicated, just as my life was less complicated ten years ago than it is now. Prayer perhaps came more easily then.

I remember another friend in Bedford — like Steve, a man near my own age — who one day had some kind of attack on the street in New York and never regained consciousness. We weren't sure what happened; all we knew was that the police found Ron lying on the street in lower Manhattan, took him off to the hospital, and four days later he died. I sat with him a good part of those four days, along with his Christian Science wife and her practitioner, while Ron's parents waited silently and uncomprehendingly in the hall outside. It was a grim experience, and the infighting between Ron's wife and his parents was almost too much to take.

The parents were numbed by the tragedy and

could only sit mutely, knowing in their hearts that their only son was going to die. Betty, however, kept up a cheerful front. "Of course, he can hear me, John. He's just sleeping now to get some rest before he wakes up. Ron, you know I'm here, don't you?"

What was I supposed to do, play her game and pretend that nothing, nothing at all was wrong?

I was caught between Betty, whom I liked and for whom I felt sorry because the experience in the hospital was so distasteful to her as a Christian Scientist, and Ron's parents, whose agony made me cry inside. When Ron did finally die, mercifully, we had a funeral at St. Matthew's with Betty and the three boys (Jimmy, my godson, was three and barely able to understand what it was about). We sang a couple of cheerful hymns and kept our composure and said all the words the Church says at funerals, and I looked strong, and when it was all over I went into the sacristy and cried my heart out. For Ron, for Betty and the boys, for people who pretend, for everyone who has to die and for everyone who's left behind to pick up the pieces and start over again.

I still wear some of Ron's clothes which Betty later gave me — "dead man's clothes," my children call such gifts which come my way from snappy dressers like Ron — but wearing their clothes doesn't get me any closer to the people I want to reach, any closer to Ron or to his family. Betty said later what a good friend I'd been to them all, but three years of seminary and ten or so years in the ministry didn't help me much when it came to reaching Betty or even praying for Ron's recovery.

One afternoon about that time a man I knew slightly called and asked to come see me. It was unusual in Bedford, a commuting town, for any man to be around in the afternoon. I used to joke that the only males in town during the weekdays were the school headmaster, the antiques dealer, the undertaker, and me.

"Sure, Harold, I'll be in the Parish House. Come on over."

When Harold came into my office I was glad to see him, and not only because he was thus the fifth male in Bedford on that particular afternoon. I was glad because I liked him and because it was obvious that he was turning to me for some kind of help. Every minister wants to be needed. We're never so happy as when someone asks our advice.

I didn't wait for Harold to ask my advice, though. Instead I sailed on, talking about a school meeting we'd both been to two nights before and from there to a new road the state was trying to put through the town and which was on everyone's mind.

Except Harold's.

"I tried to kill myself this afternoon," he slowly said when I paused in my happy recital of what was going on in town.

"You what?" I blurted out.

"I tried to jump in front of a train at 125th

Street but someone pulled me back. I was so frightened at what I'd done that I ran before anyone could get to me. The police never found me. I somehow got to Grand Central and took another train home and called you from Bedford Hills. John, why did I do this? Why don't I want to live?"

School meetings, new state highways, people who work in New York City and commute an hour and a half each way every day and who see their families only on weekends, the pressures to succeed, to make money, to have a better place than someone else — Harold was caught between the demands of his family, his job, and those other demands on him as a person. For a brief moment those pressures got too much for him, as they might have for me too were I in his shoes. He was there in my office in the Parish House asking for help, sobbing out his story while I listened and wondered how I could have been so insensitive to anyone who had turned to me.

I did help Harold, I guess. I listened to him for two hours that afternoon and later spent some time with him and his wife, Ginger, trying to get them both to see what was going on in their lives. They eventually moved to another town, and when I saw Harold a couple of years ago he seemed a much happier person. I hope he is. I also hope that I'll never again let a person's outward appearance fool me when he comes to see me.

Or will I?

I'll probably do the same thing again, like everyone else who thinks he learns a lesson from some difficult experience. Because I'm human, I'll make the same mistakes. I'll bawl out someone the night before her operation when I'm fed to the teeth with her whining. I'll smile pleasantly at the Christian Scientist who tells me her husband's just sleeping and doesn't have a clot on his brain. I'll do it again, although perhaps under different circumstances, and I'll interject my own personality in some crisis when the very thing that's needed is for me to take a back seat.

We clergy like to be at the center of the stage, no matter how humble we're supposed to be. Even my father, who was a humble man, had a very large ego, which needed to be front and center a good deal of the time. People called him a saintly person. So he was. But he, the human being, was always in the center of the kind, thoughtful acts he did for others; he had no intention of not being noticed, any more than I can remain hidden as a personality when my need is to enter the lives of my parishioners, to find ways somehow of making my life a part of someone else's.

It's hard to remain hidden when you need to shine; it's equally difficult to remember lessons when you haven't been able to rid yourself of some of the same inner drives that got you into trouble in the first place.

As I sat looking out the window on Sunday afternoon, the pictures on the study wall acted as a kind of drug to keep me from dealing with the present. It was by mere chance I noticed an article in a college magazine I'd been looking at the night before. I'd only got through the first half of the article about religion at the University of Michigan when I got bored — on Saturday night too — thinking about religion, of which not many hours later at St. John's I would be the chief exponent. I'd left the article and gone to bed. Ann Arbor is probably no different from Cambridge or New Haven, except that there are over thirty-three thousand students at Michigan, and that's a lot of student-power both for good and for ill.

I picked up the article again now and came to a paragraph which, oddly, followed the paragraph where I'd left off reading last night.

Loneliness, estrangement, isolation, describe the vast distance between man and man today. These dominant tendencies cannot be overcome by personnel management, nor by improved gadgets, but only when a love of man overcomes the idolatrous worship of things by man.

It was a paragraph from the Port Huron Statement of S.D.S. in 1962, and it couldn't have better fitted my mood. Loneliness, estrangement, isolation were all part of the experiences of the day, from Linda and Michael, who are estranged from the kind of church I know, to Steve, who's isolated there in the hospital. There are vast distances between us. None of the gimmicks of religion are going to help bridge those chasms that separate us — no "personnel management" or "improved gadgets." Somehow, as the S.D.S. statement says, love has to take the place of idolatry. A lot of my religion and that of my friends is idolatry, of ourselves and our petty and often cheap religious tricks.

When we can listen — when we don't have to be front and center all the time — maybe then some of the S.D.S. ideal of love for others will come into being. I've tried the "gadgets" and I know they don't work. There has to be a better way, for Linda and Michael, for Steve, and for all the other people I know.

I got thinking about my family. One area in which religion hasn't appeared to be of much direct help is in the bringing up of my children. I don't mean we've failed. Barbie and I must have done something right, religion must have played a more important part than I realize, because we have three bright, attractive, and for the most part delightful children. Their values appear to be good ones. Debby (a sophomore at Wellesley), Jeff (who's in the eleventh grade at St. Albans School here in Washington), and fifteen-year-old Betsy, our beautiful beanpole, are all fun to be around, particularly when we're not around each other too much.

When Barbie and I were first married and when Debby came along, we tried to figure out some way of having time together as a family on weekends. Both Saturday and Sunday are obviously hectic days in the life of a clergyman, and as our children have gotten older and their weekends have come into conflict with mine, it's often seemed as though there's no chance of reconciling my schedule with theirs. We tried having family Sunday dinner on Saturday night, but it never really worked. We tried having a big meal on Sunday, either at noon or in the evening, but I'm too weary or keyed up after church, and Barbie doesn't like preparing a heavy dinner in the evening. The children don't care that much about eating one with us, anyhow.

So what happens? We go our separate ways on weekends, take long summer vacations together, see as much of each other as we can during the week. This includes a family breakfast on schooldays, which does at least bring us together for a short time every morning. I realize our family's not alone in this problem, but I keep looking for ways by which we can spend more time together. Even though I know it won't work I still feel somehow that Sunday should be such a day.

Christmas is often a disaster in a clergyman's family. He's caught between the holiday demands of his parish and parishioners, and his family. And if he's at all sensitive to the past, he has conflicting memories of these too, especially if like me he is the son of a minister. Sunday also is a lousy day for family togetherness. Unfortunately, five of the other days when the minister might take time off, the children are in school.

Where does religion come into our children's lives? Indirectly, ever since they were very little, they've known what a minister does, and to the extent that they're aware of the problems I face, they understand without having to be told what goes on in the church. Barbie comes by her faith in a relaxed, even casual, manner, so we've never made a big deal about going to Sunday School or church. We — they, the children — simply went when they were little children, and then when they got into their teens and began to rebel we let them, most of the time anyway. The result has been that Debby (who when she was thirteen used to proclaim loudly, "I'm not the religious type") has become as devout as old Mrs. Thatcher. Debby taught Sunday School for two years and is up early on Sundays when she's at home, to go to Holy Communion. No prompting on my part. She walks the mile and a half to church, and I think it's right and natural for her to be there.

Jeff likewise went through a period when he resisted going to church, and so Barbie left him home on Sunday mornings, to watch TV and play with his dog Chris. After a while he got bored and decided to share in what the rest of the family was doing at eleven o'clock. Now he sometimes serves as an acolyte and sometimes helps Marti and Bob Patchell in the Sunday School. Since he attends a Church day school during the week, he feels he gets enough religion. Probably he does. But Jeff recognizes that occasionally some good things go on down on Lafayette Square on Sunday and he wants to be a part of them. That's why he comes to church now.

Betsy became bored with Sunday School early in her church-going career. She's a bright kid and I don't blame her. But she's also got Barbie's traditionalist streak in her and something in Betsy made her stick it out for the entire seven years until she was confirmed. Now she's beginning to question some of the tenets of the Church, especially since most of her school friends are not in any way associated with formal religion. Church is now an occasion for her to count the grammatical mistakes of her preacher father or to see some of her other friends who are there on Sunday morning. Later the Church may mean something more to her.

Betsy likes to sing hymns and is a good critic both of the music and of me. Jeff mostly keeps his criticisms to himself. But I'm pleased to note from time to time that he's been listening and evaluating what he hears.

I want it that way. I want my children to speak out when church is boring or stuffy or when they see intolerable inconsistencies in me, their father. Once as a boy I was asked what part of the service I liked best. "The announcements," I said. How come, I was asked? "Because that's the time in the service I feel I can talk to my father. It's the time he's the most natural and I can speak to him."

Wow!

Debby, Jeff, and Betsy: what's your favorite part?

Where are the places in public worship when you feel the most comfortable and secure? When the prayers are said and you're supposed to be talking to God? When the announcements are given out and you feel you can talk to your father, who's acting then more like a man and less like a priest? Do you ever get the two mixed up in your mind, and instead talk more comfortably to God and with less ease to your father? Maybe you can talk naturally to both of us.

In spite of disadvantages, the clergyman's family has opportunities which can be very exciting indeed. Take travel. I've preached on several occasions in churches in Europe and it's been possible, what with free housing and excursion rates, to take my family with me. In the course of these trips I've served two English country parishes where housing was provided in the local rectory. I've preached at St. Paul's Cathedral in London, Westminister Abbey (where I received three pounds for "travel expenses") and St. Martin-in-the-Fields on Trafalgar Square. I've celebrated Holy Communion in a YMCA chapel on the shore of the Sea of Galilee. Several years ago, when I gave the concluding service at Eton, a member of the Royal Family who happened to be present was overheard to say, "Well, that was a breath of fresh air in this musty place!"

I liked that.

For four summers I have exchanged pulpits — as we say in the trade — with the Dean of the American Cathedral in Paris. This has worked well for everyone concerned, since Dean Riddle has lots of admirers in Washington who come to St. John's to hear him, and it gives the Harper family a chance to spend a month in Paris with some traveling around Europe thrown in as well. The American Cathedral on Avenue George V is a superb example of English Gothic, a beautiful, imposing church which serves as a rallying place for English-speaking people in Paris. The services are generally in English. Once, however, I stumbled through a marriage service in French while a photographer ran up and down the aisles taking pictures. Under my breath and in English because I couldn't think of the French words I growled, "Get the hell out of here or I'll bust you in the nose." Either he didn't understand English or knew I was too preoccupied remembering French words for love and honor. In any event, he won, and I was told at the reception by one of the guests that he could understand "un peu" of my words. That was about all I understood myself.

When we were first married we bought a summer home on Cape Cod. It seemed to my cautious New England parents-in-law an extravagant thing to do, but over the years the house has paid for itself through summer renting, and it has also provided our family with a feeling of permanence. It's at Cape Cod that our roots are and it is there that we return to be together as a family.

The travel abroad has been important for us all, and I'm probably a better preacher because of the exposure to different cultures and different people. Our children gain too, not just because of the travel but because of the people they meet in other places as well as those who come into our home in Washington. Unlike some children, ours have always seemed to enjoy being around guests, and people comment on the naturalness with which they relate to older people. I'd like to think this is because we've allowed them to be themselves, to join or not join with us as they wish.

And perhaps there's another advantage to being a minister's child. It may be that very early in life the child comes in contact with the great crises of human existence — birth and marriage and death. Jeff's our most sensitive child, I think, and he some-times takes the death of parishioners hard. He's not had to experience the death of close members of his family, but he's had some good training by sharing with us in the pain and loss of parishioners. Just answering the telephone in a minister's house can be an education in itself.

As a child I loved to go to funerals which my father conducted. "Morbid curiosity," said my seventh grade teacher, and she was probably right, but on the whole I think the experience did more good for my emotions than harm. Our children have standing invitations to attend weddings. Certainly they've seen enough of the sham and sometimes of the beauty of such events to give them some idea of what is wrong and what is right.

I try to be careful in what I say at home about

pastoral problems. Usually I'm discreet with Barbie and the children, but a minister's family can't help but be aware of the telephone call, the person who visits the rector in his second-floor library, the man who comes to the door and talks briefly with his minister in the front hall. I'd like to believe that in being exposed to some of this a clergyman's family itself is better able to handle the truth.

The good and the not-so-good are as much a part of my children's life as they are of mine, and no matter how hard I sometimes try I can't separate the ministry from those hours when I'm in my role as a husband or as the father of three children who need me just as much as any parishioner.

Chapter 13

LATE SUNDAY AFTERNOON Barbie opened the door to the study. "I know you're tired, but don't you think we ought to stop in for a few minutes at the Hansons' party? I said we'd come. We don't have to stay very long."

The last thing in the world I wanted to do just then was to go to a party at Rufus Hanson's house. He's the kind of man who wants his minister to look and act like a minister one hundred percent of the time, which means that when I first turned up at a party in a necktie he tactfully suggested that it was not in good taste and that when I allowed the United Mine Workers to hold a press conference in the Parish House protesting something that the White

House was up to, he sent me a barbed letter telling me why that, too, was wrong. On Easter he wears a cutaway and while he is always elaborately polite to us I know perfectly well that I am not the precise model of a rector that he desires. Nevertheless, he is a good, and loyal, friend. When he was on the Vestry he supported me at Vestry meetings and in other ways, even though he enjoyed treating me sometimes like the junior foreign service officers he was used to pushing around. For Rufus Hanson was once an ambassador to a small country no one's ever heard of, and neither he nor his wife will let you forget it.

The Hansons' cocktail party would be full of a mixture of people, some of whom I feel kindly toward and some of whom I will run from as soon as I spot them in the room.

Once when I complained to my doctor about fatigue he sneered, "Well, why in hell do you go to so many parties? Do you get more business that way? I don't go to all the parties my patients give."

Such social gatherings do provide a way in which I can keep in touch with my constituency, to use a good Washington word. Whether I like it or not, I am the minister of people like the Hansons as much as I am of the Rodgerses — or for that matter, the Bentleys, Linda's family, who no doubt would be at the party too.

Sometimes I feel like an intellectual prostitute at dinner parties. I listen to conversations about people's prejudices. In the interest of being polite I hold my tongue and don't say anything at all when I disagree entirely with what's being said. There are times when I feel like telling the whole room full of people to go to hell, but so far my record's been pretty good. I haven't been thrown out of a party yet.

Sometimes I have trouble staying awake. Once I was sitting next to a loquacious dowager at a formal dinner in Washington and she was telling me a long story. I fixed my eyes somewhere in the middle of her face so that I would appear to be hanging on every word, and I nodded and grunted at what I thought were the appropriate places while my mind wandered. Finally, she stopped and looking straight at me said, "I don't know why I'm telling you this story. You're not interested in it and I'm not interested in telling it. Why don't we just sit quietly and not try to talk for a while?"

What a lady! It was one of the dinner parties I enjoyed the most and where for a time I didn't have to say things and listen to things that made me angry inside.

Rufus and Mary Hanson greeted us with considerable warmth at the door of their house in the Spring Valley section of Washington. Naturally, I was dressed in my clerical best and I undoubtedly added some dignity to the party. After all, a clergyman, even if he does have some liberal ideas, might be of some use at such a social gathering. I'd like to have told the Hansons about how I was planning to alter the Marriage Service for the Jewish son-in-law of their proper friend Gwen Bentley, but I knew they wouldn't understand. Better wait until they come to the wedding and find out for themselves. I'd like to have told them about Steve and how I wish I could pray for him now, how I wish I could make religion useful to him when he is hurting the most. But they'd never understand that, either.

Rufus Hanson is a pillar of the church and has never doubted the existence of God, prayer, and his own good works. He'd never understand how a minister could doubt the value of all those things he, Rufus Hanson, and I, have surrounded ourselves with. I'd like to have told him about that paragraph in the S.D.S. article which, if translated into religious terms, would put the Church as Rufus and I know it out of business. But then if that should happen, Rufus Hanson wouldn't ask me to his parties. I might miss being here.

There must be a side of me that enjoys sparring with the Rufus Hansons of this world. Maybe it wasn't such a drag to end my complicated Sunday at a cocktail party in the home of people whose social values I don't really buy. Maybe I'm on firmer ground now at the end of the day. The Rufus Hansons of this world are a lot easier though to come to terms with than love and death.

Then I thought of the Irish maid I'd seen earlier today, the one I always meet on Sunday morning as I walk to church down Connecticut Avenue, the one who never speaks to me. She might have been one of those three women in black uniforms and white aprons passing hors d'oeuvres at the Hansons' party.

She wasn't, but if she had been here tonight, she would have fitted right in with the guests and the help; self-possessed, well-behaved, eyes averted from any contact with me or anyone else. The insulated people of this world. I'd met them all in various places, at a cocktail party, for instance, like this one. People who give parties, people who work for people who give them, people who come to them. Mr. Hanson, someone's maid, someone's minister — we pass each other without any kind of glance, backward or forward, not even sideward.

"Why don't you come and meet our house-guests?" Mrs. Hanson said, tugging at my arm.

I'd been trying to decide whether to have a drink from one of the trays of cocktails being passed, but since I wanted to go back to the hospital later in the evening I'd decided against it. Steve wouldn't have cared, but I did.

"Sure," I said, trying not to sound too eager or too willing to be Mary Hanson's captive clergyman. "I'll be happy to meet them."

The couple in question turned out to be people about the Hansons' age visiting from a suburb of Cincinnati, and I could tell by the way they greeted me that they were not only Episcopalians but professional ones at that. They were comfortable being around a minister and they had the Church's lingo down pat.

Right away Mrs. Jurgens told me that she and her husband had been at St. John's eleven o'clock service with the Hansons.

"Such a sweet little church!" she exclaimed echoing the comment made a hundred times a week by people who're taken with the beauty of Latrobe's building and often by nothing else. "We loved being at your service, er — Dr. Hawkins — and it was such fun sitting at last with Rufus and Mary in their pew."

Fun indeed. Dr. Hawkins! The Hansons don't own a pew at St. John's anymore, but they did once, and I'm sure it used to be a lot of fun for them and their friends.

When I came to the parish in 1963 one of my stipulations was that we would abolish the antiquated and (to me) snobbish custom of renting pews to parishioners. This practice had meant in effect that seats were reserved for those who could afford to pay for the privilege of sitting where they wanted. It effectively discouraged people of modest means who didn't feel they could aspire to owning a "sitting" from coming to St. John's at all, and also put off tourists and visitors. It just wasn't worth the hassle to come to St. John's on a Sunday morning and either be shunted to the rear of the church into one of the "free" pews, or wait until Mrs. Gotrocks was safely in her seat and then run the considerable risk of sitting next to her in her late husband's vacant place. I was prepared, though, to sit it out (a bad pun, but a true statement) for several years before freeing St. John's seats. But within six months after I'd been rector the Vestry decided the time was ripe, and we announced to a fearful parish that as of

January 1, 1964, there would be no more reserved sittings.

This didn't rock the boat as much as we'd expected. What discontent there was came from predictable quarters, from people like the Bentleys who seldom came to church anyway but who liked to feel that a place was ready for them when they did decide to worship God at St. John's. Henry Jenkins, however, was irate and went around Washington for a year denouncing the new rector of St. John's. "St. John's was the last class church in Washington," he declared, "and now it's gone." Old Mrs. Hanley, who had sat in the same pew since she was a young girl, timidly asked whether if she got to church a half hour early it might be possible for her to sit in her usual seat, and I assured her that certainly it would be quite possible. In fact, the ushers have been thoughtful, especially about older people, and while we haven't actually saved pews we have taken into consideration people's preferences.

Stewart Knower, our former head usher, once gave a talk to the Sunday Adult Forum on the topic, "I would rather be a doorkeeper in the house of the Lord . . . ," which he later admitted was stretching it a bit since he gets a lot of flak from people who want to sit in one particular place when there's simply no more room, or who give him a hard time by coming in late and demanding to be taken up to the front pew. Ushering, he reminds me, can be a hazardous business. So can the ministry, I tell him.

The Hansons were among those who went along

with the demise of the rented pew system, but not very happily. I'm sure they told their Cincinnati friends — I forget their names — that it was "their" pew they sat in this morning and they probably made a slightly disparaging comment about how times have changed from the good old days when St. John's had all the right kind of people in it and everyone knew his place. Now they even have Negroes, my dear, but mostly ones from African embassies in their colorful native dress. So interesting and colorful.

After I got over the Jurgenses' comments about St. John's beauty, "the simply lovely stained glass," the music, and then a kind word for me, Mr. Jurgens took over the conversation, and I mean took over. He'd obviously been waiting for a chance to talk to an Episcopal clergyman, and I was fair game. After all, wasn't I the Hansons' rector and used to being talked to by powerful people like Rufus Hanson and now by his friend Mr. Jurgens, Senior Warden of his parish in Ohio? Mr. Jurgens had a lot on his mind, and in the next fifteen minutes he proceeded to tell much of it to me, while Mrs. Jurgens nodded approvingly of her husband's wisdom and Barbie slipped away to talk with one of her tennis partners. It was a difficult fifteen minutes, but I was interested in what Mr. Jurgens had to say, which seemed to be a summary of all the unhappiness that many people have with the Episcopal Church in the 1970's.

"Dr. Hawkins," he began, and I decided to resign

myself to that new name. "I'm glad to see you don't use that godawful Green Book in your services, even though I regret to note that your young assistant did not read the Lessons from the St. James Version, but from some modern translation." (It's actually the *King* James Version, but never mind.)

I started to tell him that we were in fact using all the trial services that the Episcopal Church is experimenting with but that for tactical reasons we are not using the cumbersome paper-bound green Prayer Book that has aroused the ire of so many people like Mr. Jurgens. We have printed the service in a smaller booklet of a different color. Rufus Hanson, who shares the Jurgenses' prejudice against contemporary Bible translations, has nevertheless been approving of our liturgical experimentation; at least neither he nor most of the other members of the parish have raised the anguished cries that have been heard from Episcopalians in other parishes when they sense that their beloved Prayer Book is about to be altered or taken from them altogether.

We were lucky in our method of experimentation at St. John's. Most of our people are willing to go along with new styles of liturgy providing that one or two sacred cows aren't disturbed. One is the familiar sixteenth-century wording of the Lord's Prayer which many of the devout are certain was the exact form Jesus used at its inception, in the same way they find it difficult to understand that Jesus was a Jew and would be denied membership in the Chevy Chase Club if he were around today.

I decided a year ago that it wasn't worth tampering with the Lord's Prayer — after all, I'm a conservative when it comes to retaining some of those things I've grown up with — and it didn't seem necessary to me to be crucified on every cross. We've gently led normally resistant people into some new forms of worship, and people like Mr. Jurgens don't realize it but they are being exposed to something new in spite of their preference for the old way.

Mr. Jurgens didn't get his defenses up until he heard the Bible being read in blunt and clear contemporary language. He's happier to have religion detached from everyday life, more of an art form (and the King James translation is certainly that), than to allow religious rites to intrude too intimately into his thoughts about himself and about other people.

Changing the subject, Roger Jurgens continued his monologue. "We're looking for a new rector at St. Luke's," he said, informing me that he was chairman of the selection committee of his suburban Cincinnati parish and then proceeding to tell me the kind of clergyman they were in search of. For a minute, I thought he might have been propositioning me about the job, but it became apparent that anyone who allows his assistants to read from anything other than the King James Bible would be ineligible for the ecclesiastical height which was St. Luke's. Whether the rest of his committee is as conservative I don't know, but I suspect Mr. Jurgens carries a good deal of weight. He is forceful, knowledgeable, and above all loud and probably very rich. The latter two qualities no doubt help to fit him for leadership in his parish's search for a new shepherd of the flock. Mr. Jurgens would be closer to the sheepdog than to the sheep, wary of the shepherd even while at the same time aiding him in his work.

It's amazing to me that the right man ever finds the right parish, or vice versa. With the exception of the Roman Catholic and Methodist churches, where pastors are assigned by higher authority, the system in most American churches is chaotic, and everyone complains about it. There hasn't yet been found a really effective way of promoting someone whose talents are especially suited to a particular parish and at the same time allowing the congregation to have a significant decision in choosing its own leader. Mr. Jurgens told me that his committee has forty-two names it is considering, men from all over the country who must be interviewed and evaluated. Most of the people on calling committees have never been through the experience before; some want to move very quickly and choose the first name on the list; others are more cautious and enjoy dangling men on the line and watching them squirm in their eagerness to be considered for the job.

Mr. Jurgens wants an articulate preacher, but not a man who "will preach politics from the pulpit." He wants someone who is good with young people — to "bring 'em into the church" — but at the same time St. Luke's has a lot of older parishioners who need to be spiritually fed as well. Noting that I wasn't drinking, he said that it was important that a man should not be a prude, which meant to him that his minister should drink with the best of them. (I suspect from experience in these things, however, that Mr. Jurgens would be the first to howl should his new rector show any signs of having some of the human weaknesses that he and his fellow Vestry members might possess.) He wants, in short, a small, human replica of the God he worships: affable, accommodating and humble. If I told him that his God and his image of a rector are too small, he wouldn't understand my humor; in fact, God and his minister are quite big enough as it is and they'd better not get any larger.

Rufus Hanson once told me that he wants sermons to be "spiritually uplifting." I think I know what he expects, and what Mr. Jurgens expects also, and I'm uncomfortable with their desires. They want to hear about the Bible in sermons but couched in beautiful Elizabethan words, and they want to hear about an Elizabethan Jesus as well. They are selective in those parts of the Bible they will listen to and indeed they are wary of Jesus himself. "Spiritually uplifting" may simply mean having their minds put at ease rather than having their consciences pricked. You can't have it both ways, I've discovered, and so have many people who have left churches throughout America today.

I like to preach and I enjoy preparing sermons. There are some things about the ministry I don't like, but I'm excited by the challenge of trying to communicate to other people a particular point of view (especially to those who need some convincing). However, I get bogged down in writing a sermon when I think of the people to whom the sermon is addressed. There are those at St. John's, not many, who call me "Father" and who expect a churchy kind of sermon with references to "Our Lord" and to "His spiritual Body, the Church." They are good people for whom the Church is the most honest expression of divine presence that they know. They come to Holy Communion, especially to the early service on Sunday or on weekdays when they can be alone with God. They are in a literal sense pious people who fast before receiving Holy Communion, who spend a certain amount of time each day at their devotions, and who never for a second doubt the existence of God.

Then there are those who call me "Mr." or "Doctor" and others who address me as "Reverend" or "Rector," which tends to put me in a particular category from which, like the category of "Father," it is hard to escape. These people too have their expectations of the sermon. The expectation may be that it will be dull, noncontroversial, and of no earthly use to them when they leave St. John's to go to the Club for lunch. Or they may expect a sermon to enlighten them about something they don't already know. They hope their minister will in fact come up with some new trick each Sunday, and they are ready for the challenge as they settle back in their pews and wait for him to begin. Prove it to me, they say; tell me something I don't already know; stretch my imagination, my ability to believe, excite me. Like the country preacher who described his sure-fire method of preaching by saying: "First I 'spounds; then I 'splains; then I gives the 'rousal."

'Spound. 'Splain. 'Rouse. Many churchgoers demand all three of their preacher, and they feel they haven't gotten their money's worth if he fails to deliver the goods.

Finally, there are those who symbolically, at least, call the preacher by his first name. I see these people asking him to be one of them, to share their anxieties and to share his with them. And share his certainties too. Steve Rodgers is such a person. But Rufus Hanson doesn't want this kind of sermon. Sometimes when he thinks he is being funny but when I know he is deadly serious he refers to me as "My dear Rector." That's the way he would have it, and not as "dear John."

Yet Rufus likes having me around. Why? Is it to prove to himself that he is on an equal footing with the religious symbol that he addresses only by title? To tell himself that even though God may be high and holy and that His representative must be like Him, there is nevertheless the thinnest possibility that the holy can become human, the minister be turned into a man, that God's majesty may be experienced on the level of a cocktail party?

If Rufus Hanson were aware of this, he would be

on to some really good theology, for that's what the Incarnation is about: God "became flesh and dwelt among us," to quote St. John (according to the King James Version, at that). Mr. Hanson's respect for God is something he takes very seriously, and this carries over to his rector as well.

There are times when he wants to meet God in person. Like the rest of us he needs Him in ways that even a powerful man like Rufus Hanson can't fully articulate. But Steve, who's not turned on by the same things that interest Rufus Hanson or Roger Jurgens, wants to hear a sermon which is an extension of his own life, which takes off from his own everyday encounters and experiences. He wants his friend John to share with him what little understanding of life and death he may have, not to convince him of anything, not even consciously to convert him, but to enable him to think these things out for himself and to make some decisions for his own life. He wants the preacher to hold up some kind of mirror for him to look into, to see himself for what he is, and to know that the One Whom he sees has strong arms which will not shake when the rest of the foundations of life come crashing down.

He looks at me, though, and knows that my arms aren't always very strong; he looks at those who come to church each Sunday, who are convinced that the Church is the bastion of truth, and he sees too many ways that this isn't so. Steve looks at some of the people around him, at Rufus Hanson, say, and wonders whether his unquestioning faith can help him, Steve Rodgers, come to any greater knowledge of the Christian life.

I once told Steve that I've never preached a sermon more than a couple of weeks after I've written it. "Because I don't believe it any more," I said to him. I might have added: because faith for me is an ever-changing experience, and yesterday's certainties become today's doubts, and what is unclear now and of concern to me may tomorrow become the rock on which I can stand. Convictions, I tried to tell Steve one day, don't necessarily have to be unchanging; in fact they may alter considerably as people grow.

Roger Jurgens is used to having his way in his parish, and he wants to be sure that his new minister understands the ground rules. I'm not a candidate, of course, but Mr. Jurgens was trying the ground rules on me and making sure I understood too. I thought of my first two Wardens in Bedford — of Bartow Farr, who almost single-handed chose me for the job and who, after having interviewed me, took me into the bedroom of his dying wife. Just before we entered he said to me in his quiet way, "Well, I guess you're going to be my pastor, and Selma and I need you now."

And of Lawrence Cabot, the Junior Warden, who told me soon after I went to Bedford that I was going to have to earn his respect and support. "Don't think you can play as hard as we do; drink as much; live the way we do. You can't, and you'd better get that straight. You're here to promote religion, to save our souls."

He and Bartow Farr were different men, Bartow humbly asking for help for himself and his dying wife, Lawrence making sure I knew my place and that I understood his rules and my place in his life.

Yet some years later when Lawrence Cabot's own wife suddenly died, he came to me and sobbed out his loss, the sixty-five-year-old man who had once so intimidated a thirty-four-year-old new rector now asking in his gruff way for my help. A minister is privileged to enter people's lives in so many ways, seeing them at their best and at their worst, and the intimacy of the pastoral relationship is very precious.

When I went to Bedford one of the formidable older women in the parish came to call on us, and as she left she said rather imperiously: "Since you're going to be my rector" — she might have said, Since we're stuck with you, we'll have to make the best of it — "I would like you to call me by my first name." And for all these years I've continued to do so, although Barbie and I are still embarrassed sometimes for fear others will think we're social climbing or achieving intimacies that Lawrence Cabot said we shouldn't. But Marjorie asked us to be familiar — to that extent, at any rate — and we were grateful for her acceptance of us.

I suspect Roger Jurgens will ask his new rector to call him by his first name. He will hope that the man may see him as a friend, providing the friendship doesn't interfere with Jurgens's need to play

God and for the rector's need to challenge him. Together they will discover that God is neither one man or the other and that there will have to be some compromises made if the work of the parish is to get done.

Chapter 14

ⅩⅩⅩⅩ

Some people, like Linda's mother, have a hard
time articulating what the Church exactly does mean
to them. People need reminders of a world which is
more stable and secure than the one we now know.
The Church with its familiar hymns, its aesthetic setting, its verbal and visual reminders speaks to us of
the good things which much of the time are illusory
or totally lost in our lives. Jesus is Guide and Friend,
the Elder Brother to many people in their daily
struggle for human integrity, and in some undefined
way He was originally responsible for the organiza-
tion of the Church even though He may have nothing to do with it now. The Church, for many who
take it casually, is one voluntary grouping among

others, a society of people who have a good deal in common. Which is to say that the Church can be a club for like-minded people, whose members can take it or leave it, use it or not as the spirit moves them.

Last year at a Vestry conference at St. John's I overheard Tim Simmons, our youngest and most earnest Vestryman, discussing the need for more social life in the parish with Dr. Carlton M. V. Singleton, who as a young man went to seminary for a year and never lets you forget it. He learned enough in two semesters to make him an authority today on what he likes to call "spirituality in the Body of Christ." The only thing Tim Simmons and Dr. Singleton have in common is that they're members of the human race and parishioners of the same church, and it has become apparent to me, as well as to them, that their view of the parish is completely different. St. John's is really two parishes, and if each man had his way the other St. John's would be eliminated or else consigned to a section of Washington other than Lafayette Square.

Tim was going on about how we ought to have more coffee hours, church suppers, get-togethers within and outside of the church. Dr. Singleton was appalled.

"Why, I have all the friends I can deal with as it is," he said to the younger man. "I simply don't have time with my busy schedule to give the church any more of my energies than I now do. John got us here for this Vestry conference on a Saturday morning much against my — and I might add, sir, my wife's — wishes. I'm sure it's valuable to spend some time with the Vestry, indeed, ah, to get to know a newcomer like yourself, Simmons. But really, church suppers, why that's too much!"

Tim was as upset and hurt by Dr. Singleton's lack of concern for the newcomer as the busy doctor was at Tim's seeming naïveté. Tim chose St. John's when he came to Washington to work on Capitol Hill because he believed it would be a good place in which to make friends as well as to worship. He takes very seriously the idea of the church as a community — indeed as a family — and it is a good deal more to him than Sunday morning worship. He and his pretty wife Betty organized a youth group for teenagers, but it has not been a success, through no fault of theirs. I can't even get my sixteen-year-old son Jeff to have anything to do with it, in spite of his affection for Tim and Betty. They keep at it because such church involvement fulfills a legitimate need in their lives, that of Christian fellowship with other human beings.

Tim's not the only person at St. John's who is looking for friends. As a matter of fact, I'm not entirely fair to him when I suggest that that's what is at the bottom of his wish for church suppers and youth groups. He sees the Church as the community where people can honestly interact with each other, a kind of ecclesiastical sensitivity group, and he finds that worship, no matter how beautifully it is done, is barren without some sort of significant human exposure of one life to another. He also knows that people are lonely for friendships and that this is why many in a city like Washington find their way to St. John's in Lafayette Square. He sees our women's groups as essentially a way by which many single and a few married women can meet together once or twice a month to have some companionship as well as perform services to the parish. He regards occasional men's dinners in the same way. The church is empty for many like him without these experiences, and Tim has been after me, and after other members of the Vestry, including his antagonist, Dr. Singleton, to do more to make St. John's a fellowship of people and not merely a museum or a place where people come on Sunday and go away no different than before.

Neither Tim nor Carlton Singleton would put it in these words, but both want the church to be the experience where the issues of love and death are met. Only each has a different expectation of how those issues are experienced. Tim wants to talk about them in terms of his own and others' lives, to live them out, so to speak, existentially; Singleton wants to be reminded of them through art in its various forms, music and poetry and Elizabethan language, and occasionally through a sermon. He prefers to view them dispassionately from a distance, certainly not personally in terms of his own life or those around him.

Singleton's not a coward nor is he generally dispassionate when it comes to considering the great themes of human existence. He is instead a very private person who prefers not to reveal himself in front of people he does not know or who appear not to be his kind of human being. The Church is a place to sort out his ideas, his dreams, and his fears. But it is a private place for him. Yet he and his friends are on the whole the ones who keep a church like St. John's going. They contribute generously to their church, despite their other obligations, their own group of friends, their charities. For the church really goes beyond these other activities. Like an umbrella on a rainy day it arches over the joys and pains, the victories and defeats of their lives. The Singletons help to make this kind of church possible for Tim.

The umbrella needn't be held too closely, though, and that's where people like Dr. Singleton part company with Tim and some of his younger friends. Tim and his contemporaries have their other interests, their friends and causes, but many of these, especially friends, tend to be within the church. They too want the church to be an umbrella overarching their lives, but they want the church to involve all aspects of human experience, and this includes politics and social issues no less than strictly spiritual ones.

Tim's always after me to preach about the war in Vietnam and Watergate, to talk from the pulpit about abortion and substandard housing; these, he says, are the legitimate concerns of Christianity, not just in a general, but in a very specific way. He wants to hear about them from his minister on Sunday and from his fellow parishioners at other times. He sees a legitimate place for controversy, rather than consensus or peace, within the parish, and the church doesn't interest him very much when it ducks the issues with which society in general is wrestling today. Spirituality means one thing to Tim and quite another to his fellow Vestry member, Dr. Singleton.

I'm not sure how to reconcile the two points of view. I'm not at all sure I want to. I want to keep Tim in the church and not have him give up in despair. I'm on Tim's side much of the time, even though most of the people I see and listen to can't comprehend what he's talking about.

I say I'm on Tim's side. But if I am, why don't I come out and say so, preach the kind of sermon he wants, march in protest demonstrations, lead gutsy discussion groups about social, economic, and political issues? Why don't I tell Dr. Singleton and his friends that they're wrong?

Why not? Because there is just enough validity in their position to make me cautious about denouncing them. That's why. There are necessary dark places of human existence that I can't presume to expose. Maybe the Church should be a "haven of blessing and peace" — the one institution in society which is not always in a state of upheaval or drifting with every breeze that blows from the right or the left. Perhaps there should be quiet harbors of rest and renewal, and there are occasions when the Church should be one of them.

I used to get angry when I saw people in church on Sunday not taking any visible part in the service, not singing the hymns, and staring off into space when others were reading together from the Prayer Book. Is it because they were too proud to sing or to participate with other people? Or is it because there are other ways of worshipping than doing what everyone else is doing? Is it possible to sit or to stand, and simply take it all in — like viewing a sunset without having to say something every two minutes to a companion who shares its beauty with you?

Tim Simmons wants to discuss his experiences of God; Carlton Singleton prefers not to put into words or into actions his interpretation of divine presence. Providing he doesn't tell me his is the *only* way of worshipping or being a part of the Church, I see Carlton Singleton's point. Tim, for all that I agree with him, has got to understand Dr. Singleton's need for privacy and peace one hour in the week, and let Dr. Singleton remain mute in his pew in the darkened church. Tim can and should lead the march to the White House and the Capitol, to the ghetto, to wherever human need is flagrantly exposed, and I pray that I have the courage and the will to go with him. Let him fight against sham and hypocrisy, hopeful that something better than what we now know will come along. Tim will help some of us, and Dr. Singleton should be grateful that a better world may result. It won't be the world he now knows or is at home in. But Tim will nonetheless help to bring change to the Church and an older generation may discover a new kind of Church in which the activism of Tim and the passive appreciation of Dr. Carlton Singleton both have their places.

If I didn't hope that this might come about I'd leave St. John's and get into some other work. But I do believe the Church can still be large enough to include two points of view. I myself want to be a part of the leadership of such a parish even though I know from past experience what the leadership will cost me both as a man and as a minister.

St. Mark's, Foxboro, where I began my ministry as rector, was a parish big on fellowship, church suppers, and the rest. It was a small community where people knew one another, and when Ralph Lombardi was being operated on for cancer, half the parish turned out to pray for him one evening in the church. It was a parish where the annual picnic involved everyone, the old as well as the young, not just sitting around on the grass but running in the three-legged races and sharing each other's fried chicken. It was a congregation which took its Parish Meeting seriously, to the point that it lasted four hours one time and we fought and bickered with each other until after midnight.

St. Matthew's in Bedford was different. "Heavens! No parish suppers here," exclaimed one well-heeled parishioner. No coffee hours, no anything that can touch our lives beyond the cordial exchange of greeting as one entered or left the church. But coffee hours did come after I had been at St. Matthew's a year or so. Even an annual Parish Dinner (at the civilized hour of 7:30). Even a parish picnic. I didn't do it all; the Tim Simmonses of that parish helped to bring about these changes. For some in that aristocratic parish the church became more than a spiritual way station on the road to heaven or to Manhattan; it became for many what it had always been for a few, a place to encounter another human being on the deepest level possible, in those experiences where love and death are discussed, where they are actually met head on.

And St. John's? I don't know whether these are the issues that can keep us together or whether it will only be the superb music on Sunday or the stained glass windows or an agreeable, graying rector. I'm too close to my own fears concerning love between people and the death of those I care about to be certain of where St. John's is today. St. Mark's and St. Matthew's faced some of these issues; I hope St. John's will too.

There's a hopeful sign. One of the programs St. John's has developed over the past few years is an outreach program into the community. Tim has been a member of this committee. His current interest is in establishing a blood program so that St. John's parishioners can get as much blood from the Red Cross as they need when they are sick. Tim's trying to get one hundred donors, and as of Saturday seventy-three people had signed up to donate a pint of blood apiece.

I'm glad we're into this. Besides believing in the

Red Cross Blood Program I see it as a way that St. John's can actively participate in human need within the community. That St. John's own parishioners will benefit from it is an added incentive for us to be involved. Like our parish's investment in low-cost black housing, our support of agencies such as the Kingman Boys Club, a day-care center, a community house in the ghetto of Anacostia, and a half-way house for drug addicts, the blood program gives an outlet for people's desire to help others, by giving both time and money.

It's important for us to be personally involved in these programs of good works; people like Gwen Bentley and the Rufus Hansons of St. John's should be working directly with underprivileged kids or their parents to become aware both of the needs and the opportunities.

But even this isn't as simple as it looks. I discovered recently that Rufus Hanson gives the equivalent of one day a week as a member of the board of directors of a community center on Capitol Hill. This is a different kind of involvement, but a legitimate one. I assumed when I first heard about it that Hanson merely sat on a board of white, middle-class directors who meet once a month to hear some executive report on what the agency is up to. To my surprise I learned that he, as head of the agency finance committee, spends one day each week working in the business office of the community center, putting his special talent in financing to work in that way. I'm impressed that a man as busy as

Rufus Hanson has fitted this into his schedule. He may be doing what he's doing for the wrong reason, he may not want to touch too closely the people he's helping; he may have only a paternalistic view of such a creative agency as I know that one to be. But he does give it his time, his concern, and best of all his particular talents. It would probably be a waste for him to tutor a child one night a week — Tim's lots better at that sort of thing anyway — but it is no waste for him to set up good bookkeeping arrangements and supervise the work of the staff. Maybe that's where he can best serve. For this I'm proud of him; maybe something of what St. John's really is has got through after all.

Chapter 15

O<small>H, J</small>OHN, you were so good to visit Father
yesterday," said a voice behind me at Rufus Hanson's party. It was Glenn Berryman, a middle-aged
spinster in the parish who for the last eight years has
been taking care of her aged, increasingly senile
father. The Berrymans are old friends of Barbie's
parents, and we had known them before moving to
Washington. I remember Mrs. Berryman well; she
was an erect, pillar-like woman who reminded me
of my own mother, and I suspect she had the same
kind of righteous hold on her family that my mother
possessed on ours. Mr. Berryman was a charming,
relaxed man when I first knew him, the darling of
children and pretty women and always in great de-

mand at parties. Neither of the Berrymans, as it happened, had a cent, but because they were so well liked in Washington their friends gave them money to keep them living in the style to which they'd been accustomed.

What a style it was! Mrs. Berryman was still considered one of Washington's successful hostesses, even though the people she gathered around her were for the most part slightly faded — just as she and her husband had become party-worn over the long years. It didn't matter that the parties were in actuality paid for by the people who attended them; they got their money's worth. The Berryman house on Foxhall Road was a center for Washington gossip, and in a city where gossip is a major industry the Berrymans' house was a veritable factory.

Glenn, their only child, lived with her parents in an existence which for anyone else might have been irksome but which for her was sheer heaven. She basked in her parents' popularity. The near-great who came to Foxhall Road for tea and cocktails and Sunday luncheons never ceased to enthrall Glenn Berryman. For thirty years she acted as a kind of assistant hostess to her mother, gladly carrying out orders, adoring her father's attempts at humor, and happy to be a part of such a seemingly splendid crowd of luminaries.

And then Glenn's mother broke her hip. Confined to bed in her home for what was expected to be an uneventful recuperation even for an eighty-year-old woman, Mrs. Berryman caught fire while smoking a cigarette and literally burned to death before anyone could rescue her from her bedroom. It was a hideous end for a gracious lady, and it was the end of the parties on Foxhall Road. Glenn found a small apartment for herself and her father on Columbia Road off Sixteenth Street, in quite a different sort of neighborhood from the grandeur that they had known for so long. Again friends pitched in, and Glenn moved her grieving father into what was to become his last home in Washington.

I used to stop in to see him as often as I could, for I knew from experience with other older people something of Myrick Berryman's loneliness. Glenn and the generous friends from the past did their best, but it soon became apparent that Mr. Berryman was slipping, that the close relationship he had had with his wife was what had kept him going.

Within a year after Mrs. Berryman's death, Glenn began to talk about having to move her father to a nursing home, a move she dreaded because her father was just alert enough to plead with her never to leave him. She and I talked often about the possibility, which I myself felt was an inevitability. Meanwhile Glenn was more and more becoming a recluse, tied to the needs and the increasingly querulous demands of her aging father. Finally, the decision was made to move him next week to a nursing home in Silver Spring, and Glenn and the family friend and lawyer had gently told Mr. Berryman on Friday. I was asked to follow up their conversation with him on Saturday, and so I stopped in to see Mr. Berryman on my way home to dinner last evening.

"John," he began right away in what was for him an unusually clear and lucid conversation, "do you know what Glenn's doing to me?"

I began to wonder just how senile the old gentleman was after all. He seemed perfectly clear in remembering a conversation of the previous day which I had thought would be completely forgotten.

"She's going to move me away from here to — I forget the name — but to some kind of home where I won't have any friends. Please, John" — and then Mr. Berryman's voice broke — "don't let her do this; don't let her take me away from here. Glenn's all I have left, now that Maude is gone. She promised me she'd never leave me. Please don't let her do it. Make her keep me here with her."

What could I say? Mr. Berryman was becoming too difficult for Glenn and the two nurses to handle, and besides, the money from the generous friends was running out. I knew how much Mrs. Headley and the Hansons had already given to keep this new establishment going and I also knew that unless they and the others continued their same level of generosity there was no possibility of maintaining Mr. Berryman in these surroundings. He could, on the other hand, afford the care in the nursing home; it would be easier on Glenn and in the long run might be easier on him.

I felt sorry for Mr. Berryman because I think I understood that even with advancing age and the senility that was overtaking him, he was alert enough to know that this would be the end. The wife he adored had left him, and now his daughter was about to desert him too.

"Mr. Berryman," I shouted at him, "Glenn's trying to do what she thinks is best for you. You'll be happy there, and Glenn and the rest of us will go and see you often."

But will we go to see him in a Silver Spring nursing home more often than for just an occasional visit when our consciences tell us we can't stay away any longer? Mr. Berryman in his small apartment can at least meet us with some kind of personal dignity among furnishings and pictures which are a part of his past. He can offer us a drink in glasses which were once in the Foxhall Road house, and he is still surrounded by all those other reminders of a long, and until now happy, life.

The nursing home will be different. No matter how hard Glenn tries to make him comfortable there, Myrick Berryman will soon become disoriented in alien surroundings; no matter how thoughtful the staff at the home will be, sooner or later Mr. Berryman will decide to stop living. The memory of Maude will overwhelm him, the loneliness for Glenn's constant companionship will be more than he can endure, and somewhere inside Mr. Berryman's fragile brain he will decide that life's not worth living. The evidences of old age have already taken hold of him; it's just a question of time before he himself cooperates with the inevitable process of death and decides that it's no longer worth the fight.

And Glenn? What choice does she really have, I ask myself as I meet her this afternoon at the Hansons' party and receive unnecessary thanks for visiting her father yesterday? I remember his frightened plea to me: "Please, John, don't let her do this; don't let her take me away from here."

"Father's accepting this quite nicely," Glenn proceeds to say to me, while I stand there in dismay.

"He's really quite pleased about the move and agrees it's for the best. You must have said just the right thing to him. When I came in last night after your visit he was so quiet, and he even seemed happy. I'm so glad you saw him, John; glad you were able to convince him it was the right thing to do."

Me? I didn't convince Mr. Berryman of anything; I didn't convince myself either. I simply heard a lonely old man cry out in a kind of confession to someone he knew would listen but who would neither condemn nor approve. I was privy to the inmost anguish of a father who thought he was being deserted by his daughter, by his past and all that it meant to him. When he had said these things to me and knew I had heard them, Mr. Berryman's mind closed to any further pain. He will never again tell Glenn what he really feels, and for that matter I doubt he will ever again discuss this with me. The old man will go quietly to Silver Spring, the pleas and tears over and done with. I alone will know that the pleas and tears were stronger than the apparent acquiescence that Glenn has come upon. I know what others do not know: that an old man has given one last cry for help and that there was no reply for him. Mr. Berryman knew yesterday that I could not help him, but he also knew that I, his minister, was someone to whom he could speak.

Tonight Glenn is relieved that her father is willing to leave their apartment and be taken where he will be alone. There's no use in my saying anything to Glenn about how her father needs her now more than ever, that for these next weeks she should spend as much time with him in the nursing home as she can, gradually tapering off her visits. I won't tell Glenn what I know her father really feels. She can't bear any more herself, and I have no right to intrude into her life, especially when she wants to believe what she dimly suspects is a lie. She knows her father is not reconciled to leaving their home. Glenn cannot reverse the process of age or the fact that she has no other choice. Like her father she too has to insulate herself from inevitable pain.

I speak to Glenn tonight. I tell her that I understand how difficult it is for them both and how happy I am that her father is taking it so well. We smile together in our little conspiracy.

Yes, everything will be all right, as the shadows lengthen for Mr. Berryman and the evening comes. In time the longing for Maude and for Glenn will be shut out for good, and all those fears which have surrounded him for so long will be ended. Everything then will be all right, because Mr. Berryman won't have to struggle any longer. Glenn and I can meet at some other cocktail party and tell each other how glad we are he's at peace.

There are older people who have no daughter or son to make decisions in their behalf. Nursing homes and hospitals are filled with the forgotten and the lost. There was "Uncle Dennis," as he was known in Washington, a delightful old bachelor who lived alone at the Cosmos Club and, until he developed cancer, was in great demand at parties. But then he went to the hospital and those last three weeks of his life were the loneliest of them all. His friends — elderly contemporaries — stopped coming because the ravages of cancer made them too uncomfortable to be around him. His pain was so intense that Uncle Dennis was partially drugged most of the time anyway. But he seemed to know me the last time I visited him. I felt as he reached for my hand he was reaching for the touch of one last human being before he died.

Or old Mae Rollins, who used to do sewing for us at the church and who would barge into my office and talk so loudly about her personal life (she was deaf; her listeners were not) that everyone in the Parish House came to know her most intimate secrets. But Mae didn't care; she lived alone in a third-rate hotel and was glad that someone else took an interest in her affairs.

Our interest wasn't enough, as it turned out, although we tried to keep in touch with her when she periodically went to the hospital for treatment of the malignancy that she knew would eventually kill her. She was in church in her usual seat in the front row for several months last winter, and I began to think that Mae would outlast us all. As a matter of fact, I took her presence in church for granted after a while. Even though she hadn't been to see me in the office for some time, offering to do sewing as well as tell me of her troubles, I assumed she was doing all right.

One day last March I received a call from a social worker at the Hospital Center. Mae had died there three days before and they'd been unable to find any family or anyone responsible for making funeral arrangements. It took that long — three days — to find anyone who might be responsible for Mae's wasted body. In this case it was me they called. On her bedside table in the hospital ward was a copy of our weekly parish *Leaflet*, and the social worker, after failing to discover any next of kin, had turned to her minister. Could I unravel the mystery of Mae Rollins's life?

There wasn't any mystery, I told her; none at all. Mae was an old widow who, as I knew full well, had no family; St. John's was her only family, and one that she loved very dearly. We were all she had. She had gone to the hospital a week before and died there alone and we never knew she was ill. It wasn't our fault that Mae had no one with her when she died or that her body had lain in the hospital morgue for three days before an alert social worker tracked me down. It wasn't our fault that Mae no longer had a husband or any children or that she was old and no one besides us at St. John's cared for her. It wasn't our fault that the rundown hotel where she had a room didn't think to tell me she had taken a taxi one gray day and checked in at the hospital; they didn't know she was that ill and even they didn't know when she died.

We blamed ourselves when we learned of Mae's death. So, partially in guilt and partially out of genuine affection for her we planned a grand funeral. The three clergy of St. John's all had a part in the church service, and five women friends sat in the pews as mourners. In a sense we were all mourners, for Mae and for ourselves.

It was a snowy day, and I had arranged for Mae to be buried in the parish-owned lot in Rock Creek Cemetery. I went alone in the hearse to the cemetery, and there the undertaker and I buried old Mae in a grave which is shared by other St. John's members. As I read the words of the service — "Unto God's gracious mercy and protection we commit you" — the snow began to fall in earnest, and the single wreath of flowers sent by our church ladies' group was soon covered in a thin blanket of white. The undertaker and I stood by the gray and cold and desolate grave of the woman who had died without anyone even noticing that she had gone.

On the way back from that wintry grave the hearse got stuck in one of those monstrous traffic jams which afflict Washington whenever there is the slightest amount of snow at rush hour. For two hours the undertaker and I sat silently in the stalled hearse. Finally I decided to get out and walk the mile back to the church even though I was in my vestments. Down Sixteenth Street I trudged, covered by my black cape, until I came to the warmth of St. John's.

Then I noticed that my vestments underneath the cape were wet from the snow, and I looked down and saw the reason. The button in the middle of the cape was missing, and I hadn't noticed; just in the way Mae the seamstress had been missing and we'd not known until it was too late. Mae would have taken care of that missing button at once for me, but as it was, I was wet through now and could only remember the faithful little woman I'd buried that afternoon and of how she and Uncle Dennis and my father had died alone, and that some of the buttons which hold things together will have to be sewed on by other people now.

Once a year the Christian Church remembers by name those who have died during the past twelve months. All Saints' Day, November first, is the special day set apart to commemorate these people, and while Christians sometimes get confused about the name "saints," the idea is to remember all sorts of people and not just those we associate with unusually good qualities. We conduct approximately twenty-five funerals each year at St. John's, and when I read the list of names at the service on November first I'm always struck by two things.

One is the names of those I've known well and whom I genuinely miss; the other is the names of people I don't remember at all. Looking back over the ten years I've been rector of St. John's, I'm reminded of these two facts again.

Probably a third of those who died have been closely identified with the parish and with me; another third I recall but not well; and a third I can't remember at all and may never have known. It's the last group — many of them older, single people whose funerals were attended perhaps only by an undertaker, maybe a distant relative, and a clergyman — which makes me stop and think about the meaning of death and of its loneliness for many people.

A month ago when I conducted the All Saints' Day service we read the names of twenty-three people. One was a ninety-six-year-old general whose wife is still living. Until a year ago the general and his wife kept house together, and I would drop in every once in a while to have tea with them. They grew old together, gracefully, but when General Millwood died Mrs. Millwood fell apart, and it's only a question of time before she dies in the nursing home where she's now bedridden. Next year I'll probably read her name on All Saints' Day.

Another name on the list was a young husband whose marriage had been performed at St. John's less than a year before by one of my assistants. Louis was killed driving his car to meet his wife at the office where she worked. John Turnbull, who had married the people, should have conducted this service, but he was away. I took his place at the funeral home in Alexandria. On top of the casket was a picture of the bride and groom as they left St. John's Church on their wedding day. It was another rather pathetic way of reminding us not to forget.

Yet another name I read this year was of Ruthie, an alcoholic. When Ruthie was on the wagon she was a fervent attender at St. John's. She was a lovely person, but after her only son was killed a year ago in Vietnam, she decided it wasn't worth fighting any longer.

Maybe there were six other people I knew well. The rest were simply names and they will continue to be names to most of the members of this widespread city parish. They may or may not have families to remember them, but for the family of the Church some are already forgotten because the Church is made up of people like myself, of men and women who are involved with the living and who can hold just so much in their closet of human memories.

Chapter 16

WHEN I RETURNED from the Hansons' party there were two telephone messages on the hall table. Jeff and Betsy provide good answering service for us when we're out in the evening. Jeff's wording tends to be more cryptic and Betsy's more flowery, as the first note indicated.

"Father Samuelson called you, Dad, at 7:10 P.M. and would like you to call him back this evening any time before 10:00 P.M. Love, Your daughter, Betsy Harper. P.S., I think he's a very nice man. P.P.S., You're *so* handsome."

Betsy and I have a little litany that goes on between us: "You're so beautiful," I say. . . . "You're so handsome," she replies. And then a big squeeze (a bear hug we used to call it) and lots of giggles.

I was glad she added the bit about liking Father Rodney Samuelson, our Roman Catholic priest neighbor, because I enjoy him too. He's been enormously kind to me and to my family. But he can be wily, in a friendly way, such as the time he preached at St. John's and just before the sermon I announced that the offering would be received "for the work of this church." He said later he missed the "t" in the adjective, got up in the pulpit and thanked me for the money that would be forthcoming for "his" church.

Sly one.

I knew what he was up to, so I told him I'd split the offering. Next time he preached, I said under my breath, when I announced the offering, "And none of it's for you, my friend!"

We lunch together regularly to talk about our work. I've learned something from Rod about the dedication that a Catholic priest brings to his ministry, a dedication which at times makes me very humble indeed. He works hard, and in a very real way the church is his family. I am luckier than he is, in a different way.

Rod Samuelson has a great sense of humor, and he can laugh at himself and at his Church as readily as he can make fun of his Protestant minister friend on Lafayette Square. Last year when I was a patient in the hospital he brought in a large bottle of Beefeaters Gin hidden in a huge floral arrangement, saying he thought I needed some "holy water," and on our birthdays last summer he had a surprise dinner party for us and arranged to have our children and some of my staff present for what was a wonderfully happy evening of good fun. That's the way he is.

Rod's not too sure sometimes about my more relaxed interest in ecumenical affairs; his background is somewhat more rigid than my own and he's finding changes in his own Church sometimes confusing. But he himself is open and generous, and I always feel when I'm with him some of the breadth of his Christian charity and the friendship which I know is very real.

Thus when I returned his call on Sunday night, which I did even before looking at Betsy's second message, I knew I would be talking to a friend who regards me both as a fellow minister and in the best sense as a brother in Christ.

That was precisely why he called me, as it turned out. His aged mother, who had been terminally ill for a long time, had finally died earlier in the day. It was, of course, a release for her and for her family, and as Rod said, Sunday was a wonderful day to go to heaven. I wondered about that. While theologically Sunday is a great day to die, death on the Sabbath does rather complicate the life of a clergyman. At least it's about all I can do on Sunday to conduct services and visit the sick in the hospital. Dying demands additional effort from the clergyman; Monday's a better day for that, or Tuesday.

Rod was calling to ask if I'd be willing to take part in the Mass for his mother. While I knew he didn't exactly expect me to do very much in the Catholic service — he's not *that* liberal — I sensed that he wanted me around. It was both as a friend and as a brother in Christ that he wanted me in the chancel of his church when the prayers were said for his mother's soul. Although he didn't put it that way on the telephone, I knew this was what was in his mind. He didn't care whether I was Protestant (or Jewish, for that matter), he cared that I share in what for him was the great spiritual experience of the transfer of life into death and into life again.

As I hung up and started to read the second of Betsy's telephone messages, I thought of what the Catholic Mass would be like, of how I'd probably be like the Maine sea captain who, when asked what he'd do in a Catholic service, replied, "I'll just rise and fall with the tide." The words aren't the important part of a funeral any more than the words I will speak at Linda Bentley's wedding to Michael Laskey are all that important.

For some people at a wedding or funeral, words do indeed have real symbolic importance. The setting, the presence of family and friends, count for a lot, too. But the love that Linda and Michael bring to each other, and that which I and others of Father Rod's friends will bring to his mother's funeral, will count for so much more than whatever words we or the Church may use. The setting, our presence together, the caring which people show to each

other will all be small intimations of what our faith
really means.

The second telephone message was more complicated than the first. In its own way it was about
faith too. In this case it was more about the commitment people make to one another. I was to call the
long-distance operator, Betsy said, in Connecticut,
and I recognized the name as that of a boarding
school which one of our parish boys was attending.
It took a while to get the call through to Gordon
Saxton, who in September had gone away to school
for the first time. I'll call the school St. Luke's, although that's not its real name. It is a church school,
however in that it has an official relationship to the
Episcopal Church, and mainly because of that I was
able to help get Gordon a scholarship.

Neither Gordon nor his parents had ever thought
of the possibility of his attending a private school or
going on to college. The Saxtons live in a modest
two-bedroom apartment in Arlington. Mr. Saxton
drives a bus. Mrs. Saxton is crippled. And Gordon,
their only son, was plodding along in the tenth
grade at Arlington High School when I began to
talk seriously with the family about the possibility
of getting him a scholarship at St. Luke's.

"Suppose," I said to his parents one Saturday
when I visited them in their apartment, "Gordon
could get his tuition paid at a really first-rate school,
how would you feel about it?"

I knew how Gordon would feel, because I'd been

talking with him on Sunday mornings as he got ready to serve as one of our acolytes. A good athlete and, from what I could tell, a reasonably good student, Gordon seemed to have natural aptitude. I wanted to do what I could to see that a potentially able boy turned into the leader I thought he someday might become. His field was too limited at home. Besides, it might be better for him to live with other boys and girls in a school like St. Luke's, where he'd have so many more opportunities than his home environment could give him.

Mr. and Mrs. Saxton were enthusiastic, although doubtful about Gordon's ability to get a scholarship which would grant him full tuition. Through the help of one of St. John's parishioners who is a long-time member of St. Luke's Board of Trustees, the arrangements were made, and he went off to Connecticut. From the beginning, letters to his parents were full of pleasure at what he was discovering, and particularly of friendships that were being made within the school community.

St. Luke's used to be a boys' boarding school, but within the last five years, along with many other independent schools, it has admitted girls, which has made for a more natural kind of community. St. Luke's seemed just right for Gordon, and I was happy to hear that he felt after several weeks that he was right for the school. His parents were proud of him, and I sensed that he was proud of himself, of the scholarship that got him there in the first place and of the athletic and even the academic success that he had already achieved.

Then the phone call. "Dr. Harper," Gordon began in a voice which did not sound like Gordon at all but like some small, badly frightened child; "I'm coming home. . . . I've been kicked out. Please, may I come see you, maybe even stay with you until I can tell my parents?"

"But, Gordon, what's happened? What's wrong? Why?"

The seventeen-year-old on the other end of the line began to cry, and it was a couple of minutes before the whole story came out. Gordon had been caught by the chaplain having sexual relations with a girl, a fellow student, in the chapel that afternoon. The chaplain had found them when he came in to get ready for the Sunday evening service, had taken them immediately to the headmaster, who ordered that both the students leave the school the next morning.

That was it. The girl, Gordon said, was someone he'd come to be very fond of and this was the first time anything like this had happened, he told me. It just got out of hand and before he knew it they were making love; then they were caught; and then they were told they must leave St. Luke's.

The chapel — Sunday — this boy with such promise — my head began to swim as I wondered what in the world I could say, what in the world I could do. Surely, I thought to myself trying to clutch at any straw, there must be some way Gordon and the girl could stay at St. Luke's. Maybe punished, but not kicked out for good. They'd done wrong. (Why in the chapel, I wondered? Did this say something about a place that Gordon hated, or maybe loved so much he was willing to risk being caught in it?) But having broken the rules, was there any way, short of permanent expulsion, they could be punished less severely?

After Gordon talked himself out, apparently resigned to coming home, and after I'd told him that, yes, he could spend tomorrow night with us and that somehow together we'd face his parents, I decided to call the headmaster myself. I've been a teacher in a school very much like St. Luke's and I know how schools sometimes lock themselves into rules and regulations and that the administration may be fearful of backing down once they find themselves in a corner. But I decided it was worth a try, and so I called the headmaster at his home. Although St. Luke's is a church school, its head is a layman whom I had once met casually years ago. I had also had some correspondence with him when Gordon was applying for admission. When my call reached him he knew at least who I was.

His first words, when I told him my reason for calling, surprised and completely chilled me. "Look, Dr. Harper," he said, "don't talk to me about words such as 'forgiveness' and 'reconciliation' and 'mercy,' none of those words, please. There's nothing I can do. Saxton broke the rules, and he's out as of tomorrow. As a matter of fact we had a brief faculty meeting after chapel and the faculty agrees this is right." (He didn't tell me then, but I found out later that the faculty was not all behind him; in fact, there were other voices besides mine which might have used words like "forgiveness" or "mercy," and which in any event urged the headmaster to move slowly.)

He went on to say that if this sort of thing was allowed to go unpunished, other schools would hear about it and St. Luke's would lose face. Morale and discipline would break down, he said, and promiscuity and God-knows-what-else could occur. No, Gordon Saxton was coming home tomorrow and he hoped that he'd never hear of the boy again.

That, so help me, was literally what the head of a supposedly good school told me on the telephone. He apparently didn't care about Gordon, the frightened inexperienced kid, nor about the girl, from whom I later learned that Gordon had already gotten into trouble in another school. The reputation of St. Luke's was at stake; rules had to be observed, morale maintained. Gordon and the girl had sinned. That was the end of it. He hoped he'd never hear of these two students again.

I hung up the telephone. Gordon is out of the school and will return tomorrow, and I'll take him over to his parents' apartment when his father returns from work. Unlike some youngsters, Gordon won't go back to Arlington High a hero who has an exciting tale of lust to tell in the locker room. He'll return a broken boy who knows he's failed himself and his family. I know Gordon well enough to be sure of this, for I think I understand some of the loneliness of this only child who, as he told me on the telephone, thought he had found the warmth of friendship he'd never known before.

Gordon's impulsive experiment to see if his love was real will lead him to lose further confidence in himself and in his ability to relate lovingly to another person. A broken schoolboy will return, having lost perhaps forever the chance to make something of himself.

It was Gordon's fault that he got expelled, and yet it wasn't. It's the fault of the school, of the headmaster, of mature men and women who look only at immediate consequences and not at the human lives that are affected. It's the fault of society, which somehow denied Gordon an appropriate relationship with his parents and friends in Arlington, which denied him up to this year so much, and then which gave him dazzling opportunities which he was unable to accept. Gordon's failure is our failure.

I don't know what I think about what Gordon did, about lovemaking in St. Luke's School Chapel. Lots worse things happen, maybe worse have happened to me on this Sunday. Maybe two adolescents' attempt to make love (what a sad phrase; to think that love must be "made" rather than be a natural part of our relationship with each other) isn't such a bad thing.

A lot is going on here of course; the breaking of

rules; the disregard for the authority of an institution; perhaps the using of one another for selfish means; the lack of respect. But there's another side which the headmaster, and for that matter I, cannot easily deal with, and I doubt if Gordon or his girl friend could articulate it either. It has to do with the way we reach each other, not as selfish human beings but as people who want to share ourselves on whatever levels there may be for us. Sex is one way. Yet even within the boundaries of marriage itself, it is a way we have trouble fully understanding or expressing.

Chapter 17

———————◆———————

MY TELEPHONING wasn't over for the evening. When the phone rang at ten o'clock I knew it would be Debby, who calls us on Sunday night. This is in addition to a weekly letter. Like every father, I hated to see her leave home for college last September. This was the first break in our family circle. Debby and I are a lot alike, and her weekly call means a great deal.

I say Debby and I are a lot alike. But of course there are differences. I became aware of this five years ago when Debby was in the eighth grade at Potomac School and was assigned a paper on the most interesting person she knew. Without my being aware of it at the time, she wrote an essay about me, and when it was returned to her with an "A" she told me about it. I asked to read it, and she triumphantly gave me the paper, proud of her grade and proud, I suspected, of her relationship to her father.

It wasn't at all what I was prepared to read, however. It was, in the literal sense of the term, a critical essay of her minister father; it showed me as I really am, faults and all, and not as the idealized parent I'd have liked Debby to see.

The essay began: "When I was little my father used to spend a lot of time with me. He made up stories and games, and he called me 'Debby Mouse.'"

So far so good.

But the first paragraph ended with quite different words: "Now that I'm grown up my father's busy most of the time. He likes to spend time with his two dogs, read, and take long walks by himself in the woods."

There you have it. What happened during the intervening years, when an affectionate father spent much of his time with "Debby Mouse," to those later years when he spends time with his dogs, alone? Debby didn't say in her essay. Instead, she chronicled the story of a man who grew up in many ways during the time his daughter was also growing, whose work became heavier with increased responsibilities, and who found his need for relaxation not with a little girl who looked to him for companionship but with a golden retriever and a mutt named Dusty and who when he was tired and irritable took long walks in the Virginia woods by himself.

Debby was not intending to be critical, but without realizing it she was. She was describing the experience of many fathers, no matter what their profession, who tend to forget the needs of their children. She was also speaking for countless daughters like herself.

I asked Debby later about that essay, and it was as I thought. She'd not intended to be unkind. She said it honestly reflected the affection she feels for me.

"But that's the way you are, Dad," she insisted.

That is the way I am, or the way I sometimes am, when a thirteen-year-old daughter, or my two other children, need what their parent has to give. No one else mattered at that moment to Debby as much as I. She described in complete candor a father who only occasionally had the time for his daughter and who was sometimes short with her even when he tried to be understanding and compassionate.

Tonight's telephone call reminded me of the busy father and now, of course, the busy daughter as well, for Debby's life has broadened from the schoolgirl to the college student who is interested in any number of people and ideas and projects. I am still one of the people who matter to her, and I know I matter a very great deal. But the chance I once had to be even closer has gone.

"Dad," she reminds me on the telephone, "I'll be home for Christmas vacation next Friday; I can hardly wait! It'll be so good to get home." Then she adds, for her mother's benefit as much as for mine, "You remember I'm going to bring Cora home with me, don't you? She can't afford to go back to California for Christmas and you said, Mom, it would be OK if she came to us for Christmas."

Cora for Christmas? I'd forgotten about the quiet, at first rather distant, girl whom Debby had brought to stay with us at Thanksgiving, her roommate at college. Cora, who comes from a broken home in Santa Barbara, the child of an apparently rich, thoughtless father who'd left her mother two years ago to marry another, much younger woman not much older than Cora herself, and Cora and her mother had had to make it on their own. Cora, who had come into our family at Thanksgiving as into a family of strangers, by the time the weekend was over had shown us what one person can do to show gratitude by simply being herself. Nothing she said expressed her appreciation to us, but it was what she was: shy, hesitant but — and this is the only word I can use — radiant.

Now Cora was to come back to us for Christmas, only I didn't want her to because I didn't want her to take Debby from us. I wanted Debby for ourselves without this other compellingly real human being, this friend, intruding into our family circle.

Debby didn't mind; she knew that Cora had no place to go. She was willing to share what is precious to her, her family at Christmas, with a new college friend. She knew that when it was over we would be glad that Cora had come, and that the same joy that Cora gave to us at Thanksgiving would be present at Christmas, too, and Debby's love for us would be shared with someone else and instead of our family being weakened by the presence of an outsider it would be enhanced.

Yes, of course I was glad Cora was coming. My "Debby Mouse" is no longer a child, and I must share her with her friends as someday I must share her with a family of her own. Perhaps too she knows that it's impossible to lose some of the love she's known, even when the love has been covered over temporarily with other demands, other needs.

Once when Jeff was in kindergarten his teacher told Barbie that she had had a funny comment from Jeff. It was when I was Chaplain of the Bedford Fire Department, and I'd recently taken Jeff for a visit to the firehouse.

"I asked each of the children," Mrs. Graham told Barbie, "what their fathers did. 'My father's a writer,' one said; 'My father's a banker' said another. Jeff said, 'My dad's a fireman!' "

No minister-father for him.

In a way, our children have always been torn between their pride in my work and their uneasiness over what my work really is. It's easier (but more dangerous) to have a fireman father, they once thought, than one who is a minister and runs a church. Firemen have specific things to do; my children weren't so sure about ministers.

I know how a minister spends his day, but once in a while I'm not sure what he's really supposed to be doing, either. I can do what I like to do best, what I think I do best, or what I consider other people think I should be doing. Often the three roles are quite different. My self-image isn't always the same one others have of me, or of any other minister. What my father did as a clergyman and what I was taught in seminary twenty years ago aren't always the same things or what I believe in today. Jeff was right. Sometimes it's more fun being a fireman.

Barbie and I are finding college for Debby expensive, just as most other parents do. Even though we're careful about expenses I come to the end of a day like today wishing my work could be free from financial anxiety so that I can concentrate on the problems of people like Gordon or Rod's mother's funeral and not have to worry now with a list of people to whom we'll give Christmas presents and how much we can afford to spend.

I live on the salary I make as Rector of St. John's, and while I'm paid well as ministers' salaries go, we have to be careful. The Vestry sets my salary, based on the demands of the parish budget, and no matter how hard we try, we always are close to the line at the end of the month. It's no different for us than for other people.

Barbie makes most of the gifts we give at Christmas, particularly those for friends here in Washington like the Hansons and the Rodgerses, Christmas cookies and perhaps some unique ornaments which Betsy delights in helping to create. There'll have to be a wedding gift for Michael and Linda, and I want it to be something especially nice so that they'll know of our friendship. Maybe we can find an old print of St. John's and have it framed as a reminder of the place where two genuinely religious people found a common meeting point, a place where they said their vows in the presence of a God who appears in a different form to each of them.

After the telephoning tonight and that call from Debby and the reminder that Cora's coming too next week, I'll briefly read the New York *Times*, which I've not had a chance to look at today, and get into bed. It's been a long day for Barbie because she's had to be a mother and housewife, as well as a clergyman's wife. It's been a long day for me, because I've had to meet people whose faith is greater or lesser than my own, whose commitment to the Church and to what I am trying to do is variable, and whose willingness to let me into their lives is not always as great as I'd like it to be.

The minister I am is a reflection of the husband and father I am. Tonight when I get into our king-size bed and turn off the light I'll think of Betsy and Jeff here in the house with us, of Debby up in Massachusetts, and of all the people who form a part of my life. And I'll be grateful for most of them, for my family and friends in the parish and on the Vestry. Like Phil Watts and the others on the Vestry; the people I work with like John and Lois and

Marti. It's been a good day even though every Sunday has its agony and defeat as well as its ecstasy and maybe its success.

For several years when I was a boy my father used to take me to Boston on Saturday to swim at the YMCA on Huntington Avenue. He wanted me to learn to swim well, to learn skills in athletics which he himself lacked. He also, I sensed, wanted us to do something together. Saturday wasn't the best day for him, what with Sunday services to prepare for, but he arranged his schedule so that we could be together, and then after lunch in the "Y" cafeteria we'd go for several hours to the Museum of Fine Arts. Neither of us was in the least interested in art, and after several visits we both agreed that the "Y" was more fun and we let it go at that.

Eventually those Saturday mornings with my father became boring for both of us. I'd learned to swim, I'd taken as many advanced lessons as I wanted, I'd passed my Junior Life Saving test. I wanted my friends to come with us to the "Y" and for a year or so I was allowed to bring one, and sometimes several, boys with us into Boston.

When that happened, things changed. It wasn't just my father and me together. While at the time I wouldn't have wanted it otherwise, I now can see that having Dougie Phinney or Henry Maskall with us on those Saturday expeditions put a different complexion on them. I don't know how my father felt about having company other than myself; he undoubtedly sensed something had changed too. But he might also have been wise enough, as I think I am now, to see that it was right for us to widen our relationship to include others, that although something was lost, other relationships were taking the place of the more simple and less complicated one between a father and his son. There had to be a place in my life for Dougie and Henry as well as for my father. In order for this to take place something important to us both had to be sacrificed.

That's what growing older meant and what it means now to Debby and Jeff and Betsy. They've always had to share me with the parish, with the people who turn to me for help and who professionally and emotionally are a part of my daily life. Now I have to learn to share them with their friends, to be thankful for Debby's Sunday night telephone calls, and for those meals when Jeff and Betsy patiently sit at the table with Barbie and me. I was grateful once to my father for Saturday morning at the "Y" and those days are still very precious memories to me. But so are the memories of shared experience with Dougie Phinney and Henry Maskall, experiences which my father made possible because he was wise enough to let me go.

When Barbie and I were married in 1953, in the town where she grew up and where her parents still live, it took three clergymen to be sure the job was properly done. One of them was the rector of the parish, another was a former rector, who had introduced us and who had become one of my respected teachers at seminary in Cambridge. The other was my father, who gave the blessing at the end of the service.

What in the world does someone give three clergymen by way of honoraria, especially when in my case I was already — as of seven days before — a clergyman myself? Money, although they probably would have found good use for it, just didn't seem like the right thing. Besides I couldn't afford to pay one clergyman, much less three.

Someone suggested giving each a present. In subsequent years I myself have received some meaningful gifts from grateful bridegrooms; a lovely watercolor of my church, a pewter mug with my and the couple's initials on it, even a cashmere sweater. In any event, I gave each of my officiating clergy a book, carefully chosen according to what I believed their tastes to be. My father's was a modern translation of the Gospels, since I knew he was forever looking for fresh interpretations of familiar words, and I knew he would put such a book to good use. I wrote in the flyleaf: "For Dubbie, on my wedding day, and with love because you're here today with us and because you're my father."

After he died two years later, I took that single book from his library and put it in mine. Like him I too look for fresh interpretation of what is worn by time and yet that which is still true. That book, with its inscription now twenty years old, is a link that still exists between us. It is a reminder for me of the

YMCA and Saturday mornings, of the kayak we once built together, of his gift to me of his own wristwatch when I went to the South Pacific during the War and of his whimsical art of service ribbons painted on the watchband when I safely returned.

The copy of the Gospels which I gave him at our wedding is proof, if I ever needed one, that I was fortunate to have a father who was also a minister and whom I had to share with parishioners even to the point of not seeing him as much as I would have liked. But he let me share in his work just the same, as I walked with him on his parish calls and in the town dump and talked with him in our home about the people he — and I — cared about.

That book now is a challenge to me for my own children, reminding me that I can sometimes walk with them and talk about some of the people, their joys and sorrows, that we share in common. I hope my father's book may someday be a gift from me to Jeff, a reminder of another father who tried to be faithful both as a man and as a priest.